SOUL RESCUE

Help on the Way Home to SPIRIT

BY: CAROLE SANBORN LANGLOIS

French Version: **ASCENSEUR POUR LA LUMIÈRE**
Published by: Louise Courteau, éditrice inc.
                 C.P. 481, chemin du Lac-Saint-Louis Est
                 Saint-Zénon (Québec) Canada
                 J0K 3N0

Original Painting by:
Ann Marie Eastburn
Copyright © 1993

Typesetting: Luc A. Sauvé
                 Montréal (Québec) Canada

Back Cover Photograph by Mark Serota

Published by:

U.S.:   **THAT'S THE SPIRIT PUBLISHING COMPANY**
                 P.O. Box 2503
                 Ft Lauderdale, Fl 33303-2503
                 Tel: (305) 522-8317

CANADA: Suite 226
                 1568 Merivale Road
                 Nepean, Ontario K2G 5Y7
                 Tel: (613) 825-0259

First Printing May 1993
Second printing revised, February 1994

Printed in Canada

ISBN 0-9637744-2-5
(previously ISBN 0-87418-304-9)

EDITED
BY
SHEILA CAPUTO

DEDICATION

This book is dedicated to the Loving Beings in the Spirit World, who have sustained me throughout this lifetime on planet earth; especially over the last twenty years, while I have been awakening as the Soul that I truly am.

1. To my **Beloved Friend, Jesus,** who has come in to talk to me on so many occasions...especially during the lowest moments of my life. A year ago, here in Florida during my meditation, he controlled my body, stood up and telepathically told me to **"follow in His footsteps"**. This I have done over the past fifteen years, through the teachings of Natural, Spiritual and Karmic Laws; as well as helping people learn to love God and themselves, which are all the things He taught 2,000 years ago.

2. To **Strong Bow,** who holds such an important place in my heart. We have walked the pathway together in many earthly lifetimes, (he was my father in at least one of them, when we incarnated together as North American Indians), and has always been there as my protector. He came in whenever I needed him, to encourage me, give me upliftment, and impart some of his wise advice.

3. To **Dr Edward Bach,** (of the Bach Flower Remedies), who assisted me for many years when I was doing

my psychic diagnosis work; until, at some point, I changed the way I did my readings. He contacted me recently through a medium, and said "we would soon be starting our work together once again, working with the medical profession", who are awakening more and more to alternative medicine, and this phenomena.

4.   To **all of the other guides** who have been in my life at some time or other, doing the specialized work needed on my bodies, to bring me to the culmination point in my mediumship and healing work.

TABLE OF CONTENTS

FOREWORD

I had lived in the same small town as Carole for approximately twenty-five years, but had never really known her personally. I knew of her and her husband as professional business people, having their office in the town. At some point, I heard through the grapevine that she was a *medium;* but that was something taboo in our area, where nearly everyone was Catholic.

After Stephane's accident and death, I started sharing all the "strange happenings" going on in our house with my hairdresser, Michelyne Vigneault. When I realized that other family members were also experiencing the phenomena in their homes, I was getting desperate as to what to do about it.

What I didn't know was that Michelyne had been one of Carole's best friends for twenty years, and with whom she shared all her experiences. Michelyne called her and explained the situation, asking if she wanted to do something about it. Carole, always considering herself "on call" to do God's work, accepted immediately. The rest is history.

When Carole came to my home, I was a little apprehensive. I knew nothing about mediums except having heard about tables shaking and things moving of their own accord. When she walked in, her beautiful energy calmed me immediately. I became like a little child, as she did a calming and healing technique through the energies, by **"the laying on of hands"**.

There is no amount of money on earth that could have paid for the experience I had, and the joy I felt, when I realized that my beloved son, Stephane, was finally free and on his way to the Heaven World. I have had a lot of joyful moments in my life with my husband and children; but the gift she gave me that day surpasses anything I could receive until I am reunited with my Stephane in our home in the Spirit World.

I will love Carole, and she will be in my prayers each day for the rest of her life. I know it will be a long one, because she is Blessed by God, and is one of His special helpers.

GAETANE GASSE

SOUL RESCUE PAINTING

When Carole contacted me by phone to do this cover for her book, we seemed to connect immediately, like old friends. Since I do art shows all over the country, this has been a whirl-wind project long distance from Florida... to New Mexico... to Canada. Thank goodness for fax machines!

In doing the first sketches after reading the manuscript, I had a pretty good idea which one she would choose, as a brilliant light flashed on the paper as I drew the hand of Christ helping the soul released from the body. We used a combination of two sketches, and this was one of them. Of course she didn't know that at the time.

When I began the work, I was "told" very clearly to place a crystal on the easel behind the painting. Never having done this before, I had to rig something up to keep it there... but it worked! I usually play music in the studio anyway, but I was told (again very clearly) to play my "ETERNAL OM" chant during this time. How wonderfully powerful! Even though my physical body was tired from many hours (of several days) of standing at the easel, it was a great experience!

The figures literally painted themselves! It is hard to describe, but many times I would just brush in the features and the entire detailed eyes – both of them looking in the same direction – would appear! This was with *one stroke* of the brush – an *IMPOSSIBILITY* under normal circumstances! Figures would "become" either male or female, seemingly by the way the paint flowed. I felt like *they* were painting *who* they were, and I was just mixing the paint, watching it happen! I feel that all of them are real people, even to the top most figure, which came out rather Indian-looking. Could this be Carole's guide, Strong Bow? Only she will know for sure. Each face has a definite personality – especially this one.

When I painted the face of Jesus, there was the most incredible flow of Love that washed over me again and again...almost too much to bear! What a joyful experience!

I have truly been privileged to do this work for such an important book! Thank you Carole, and all your "friends", who seemed to be such an active group here at the studio while I painted!

ANN MARIE EASTBURN

ACKNOWLEDGMENTS

A loving thank you to my family: Gill, my daughter Lisa, my sons Michel and Pierre, and Sylvie Bissonnette, Pierre's companion in life. My precious grand-children, Stefanie, Jonathan and Joannie, whom I adore. My brother, Don Mason and sister-in-law Michelle, who never failed to call me every week no matter where I was, to lend moral support and encouragement, and my nephew, Travis and sweet little niece Breana. My sisters Shirley Fregeau and Marilyn Sanborn, and my sister-in-law Florence Sanborn, who did such a marvelous job of raising her son Andrew alone, after my brother Ronnie returned to the Spirit World in 1977. *Andrew, we are very proud of the beautiful human being that you are!*

My love to my dear friends, Michelyne Vigneault and Simone Meloche, who have always been there for me over the past twenty years, and accepted to be my **sounding board** for everything that was happening in my life; at times, they were imperative for my emotional survival.

Deep gratitude to Mireille Cadieux-Theoret and Johanne Methot-Denis, who were with us in our insurance business for over fifteen years, and with whom I shared my Spiritual experiences everyday in the office. They believed in me, and I'll love them forever for their encouragement and loving support.

I thank my friends, Lori Ezzo, Marion Pettkus, Ron Wiggins of the Palm Beach Post and Bob Cunningham for their assistance. Mary Orr and Florence Sillano, my dear friends in the Oasis. My many friends in Canada, especially Johanne Provost who is dear to my heart. Therese Denault, Valerie Berry and all the others who know who they are. Desiree and Karen, and many others here in Florida, who were there for me; I love you all! A special thanks to my good neighbors in The Oasis Of Nurmi Isles, who were kind enough to not complain about my printer making noise, over the winters of 1990, and 1991, while I was writing this book.

DEEP GRATITUDE, AND A SPECIAL BLESSING GO TO THE FOLLOW-ING, FOR HAVING GIVEN ME THEIR PERMISSION TO SHARE THEIR EXPERIENCES.

Pierre Milot...for permitting me to use his video tape for chapter nine, and my friend Rose Grenier-Aubry, who served as the medium. Luc Chabot...chapter 4 (Monique). Nicole and Raymond Sabourin...chapter 13 (Francois). Gaetane and Guy Gasse...chapter 10 (Stephane). My dear friend Betty...chapter 8. Because of your generosity of the heart, a multitude of souls will be awakened, through the reading of this book.

A special blessing to my *Angel*, Rosa Barros, who was Heaven sent! She took over and did all the computer work after the book was completely re-edited.

I wish to thank my new friend, (although I feel I have known her forever), Ann Marie Eastburn. After looking at the work of different artists in the New Age Metaphysical Book Store in Fort Lauderdale, I knew she was the one that had to do the painting for the cover.

Lorraine Holmes, an excellent medium from Montreal, clairvoyantly told me in 1991, *that my book would be published in 1993 and a half.* You were *right on*, Lorraine!

INTRODUCTION

God and His Spirit helpers have been pushing me for several years to get this book written; but, having free will, as we do on planet earth, it seems that everything comes in its own time.

I believe there is a special timing for everything that happens in our lives. Although we have an inner knowledge that we must do this or that, nothing can happen until we have the soul growth necessary to put it all into action. Even though we are God's hands and feet on this planet, our beloved Spiritual guides cannot, or will not, force us to do anything until we are ready to do it.

My guides were becoming more insistent. They felt it was very important for humanity to understand what soul rescue is, and the fact that it even exists; for if we prepared people to leave the physical body, there would no longer be a need for soul rescue!

I am finally ready. My subconscious mind has been activated, and the words start to flow when I sit down to write. Although some of my experiences go back nine years, I remember every word and scene as if it were yesterday.

As we move into the last decade prior to the year 2000, our planet is beset with much turbulence. The time of trials and tribulations, which has been prophesied for hundreds of years, is now upon us! 1991 found many nations at war once again. Even though we on the Spiritual path wanted nothing more than peace, I do not believe there was any other choice. We were faced with a madman who wanted to control the entire planet, and was willing to go to any extreme to do so.

There is a need for a cleansing and a balancing in the Middle East, where there has been so much hatred among neighboring countries for so many centuries. This may be the only way it can occur, because conflict is all they have known for so long. I believe that, in time, out of that war will come peace and a new understanding and cooperation between all nations.

During our meditations, or moments of prayer, we can do our share by continually bombarding that part of the world with light and love. By helping to dissipate the negative energy, we may be able to help turn things around. I know that the Berlin Wall coming down so suddenly in November 1989, and the break-up of the Soviet Union that had been under the domination of communism for so many decades, happened because millions of people all over the world were meditating every day on freedom and world peace.

Humanity is really at a Spiritual crossroads. We can no longer continue on the road we have taken for so many years. We are destroying ourselves as well as our beloved Mother Earth. Most of this destruction is caused by ignorance, a lack of caring as well as greed; but the time is coming very soon when we will have to face what we have done, and take full responsibility for its restitution.

The past few years have been a time of upheavals and closing of doors in our lives, and almost everyone has touched bottom in one way or another! It was a period of cleansing and new beginnings. In our personal lives, as well as all over the globe, everything came to the surface to be cleansed and released. What a wonderful opportunity for soul growth! The real problem, however, was that the faith of millions of people wasn't strong enough to get them through these trying times. Instead they turned to a life of decadence. Turning to drugs and alcohol to escape from the reality they were living only made things worse, because they were destroying the family as well as themselves. Personally, I believe that the war turned many of us back towards God, and our faith is stronger now than it has ever been.

"Lost Souls" are souls who have passed to the World of Spirit without having acknowledged, or having knowledge of, their Divinity! If, while in the physical body, we were able to remember that we **chose** to leave our home in the Spirit World to incarnate on the earth plane to acquire soul growth, we would look forward to returning home at the end of each journey, whether short or long. There would be no fear or confusion on leaving the body, which is only the vehicle for the soul during this sojourn.

Souls are lost when they do not know, or cannot accept the fact that they have left the physical body. They are in a confused state, and wander in the fourth dimension, the one closest to the earth plane. Often, through an accident or a sudden death, they will find themselves out of the body, and don't understand what has happened to them. Many times they will go back to their homes and try to talk to their loved ones. They wonder why they can't reach them, when they are standing right beside them. They become what we call "Earthbound Spirits" and live in their own reality and space. Earthbound spirits are sometimes called evil spirits, but this is not always so. Often they are aware that they have made the transition, but are so confused that they don't know what to do, or where to go. Instead, they just hang around the places they knew best while in the physical body.

Earthbounds may wander for great periods of time in what we call the lower astral plane. Because time and space does not exist anywhere else in the Universe in the same manner it does on planet Earth, time for them has no meaning. Many people ask me why they don't just go on, and I must explain that they still have free will. Until they are ready, no one can force them to leave.

The task of many Spirit helpers is to help these souls go to a higher plane but the soul must **ask** for help or let them know that they are ready. Although the helpers are all around them in their dimension, these spirits keep their eyes on the earth plane and don't look up to where the helpers are waiting to offer assistance.

Mediums in many parts of the World have dedicated their lives to helping these lost souls by sitting in a seance room and going into a trance state several nights a week. They have allowed their bodies to be used as channels through which these souls can manifest. Many of them will not leave until they have touched the earth plane one last time, for there is something they believe must be said or they need to be in a physical body one more time. Once what has happened to them has been verbally explained, they can more easily accept their transition and move on.

The spirit helpers work very closely with these mediums, referred to as "the Light", because they are doing

God's work by helping His children find their way "home". They bring the souls to them, and are always there to receive the spirit when it has finally accepted the Light. When I started doing soul rescue work, a Spiritual guide told me that a very strong Light had been placed over my house and center, and that many lost souls would be directed there for us to help.

In most cases, when they were allowed to temporarily take possession of the medium's body, they came in experiencing their death all over again. They were feeling all the symptoms they had as they left the body, sometimes crying from sharp pains in their chest, other times screaming that their car was on fire and begging us to get them out. Each one was different, and we never knew what to expect. We had to be ready for anything.

Mediums work in different ways. Most of the mediums in England, where this work is very popular, tell the spirits that they have died, and work out the psychological impact of their passing. This can take an hour or more. Working very closely with my Spiritual guides, I prefer to convince them to go to the Light in the state that they are and let the guides take it from there. They are immediately taken to Spirit hospitals for as long as necessary and treated there. When they are ready, it is explained to them that they have made the transition. I prefer helping a greater number, even though they may have to work out the trauma in another incarnation.

Several experts on past life regression explain how we return with the memory of traumatic passings in our subconscious minds, causing problems in this lifetime. However, they can be dealt with by an expert in past life therapy. Brian L. Weiss, M.D. and former Chairman of Psychiatry at the Mount Sinai Medical Center in Miami, Florida, has written "Many Lives, Many Masters" and "Through Time Into Healing", both dealing with this subject. Robert Jarmon, M.D. and noted psychiatrist of Spring Lake, New Jersey, is also in the process of completing a book on his experiences in the field.

I believe that Spirit influenced me to work in this way because of the potential problems which may arise. If a spirit comes in who is very unhappy about being told he is no longer in the physical, he can manifest very strongly in the medium's body. It takes a strong person to control him. One of my best mediums was a young man nearly six feet tall, weighing 250 pounds. I knew that when a spirit possessed the body of a deep trance medium doing this work, I had to be in complete control physically as well as mentally, as I didn't want any harm to come to my medium's body, or to myself. A friend, who often does this work, was in trance working with one of these souls. The spirit was very unhappy and became violent. He stood up in her body and started to manifest very strongly against her six foot tall friend working with her as a control. He slapped and scratched his face, leaving marks that were visible for days. This doesn't happen often; but, being only 5'4", I prefer not to take any chances.

God is very worried about all of his children on Earth who are self destructing through drug and alcohol addiction. More and more are taking their own lives while under the influence of these poisons. Many of them pass in such a confused state that they stay in the fourth dimension. They cause problems for people still on the planet by influencing them through the mind. Alcohol and drug abuse causes a crack in the aura, making it very easy for the souls that passed over with these addictions to approach others of like mind. As "like attracts like", they can influence them to take even more drugs or alcohol until they also self destruct.

There is such a need for people to understand what is happening out there, and to learn to protect themselves from the influence of these souls. It is so subtle that, when they finally realize what is happening, it is often too late.

This book is not written to frighten people. There is nothing I dislike more than being advertised or introduced as a "Ghost Buster" when appearing on television, radio or lecturing in different parts of the country. Mankind has always been fascinated by stories of hauntings and ghosts, and the media thrives on sensationalism. Therefore, I make sure to get my Spiritual message across at some point in the program. I try to make everyone understand that we are the soul first and foremost, and how important it is that we know and accept this! We must prepare the souls for the return home to the World of Spirit, after finishing what we have come to learn and do in this incarnation. Then there would no longer be a need for "Soul Rescue".

I always tell my students that we read a **Spiritual** book with the heart, not the mind. If your soul, which is in the solar plexus area, vibrates to this information, and your "inner feeling" is that this is **"truth"** for you, then your soul is confirming that it already has this knowledge. The book is a trigger, bringing the information to the surface for your conscious mind to remember!

I pray that in sharing with you a few of the hundreds of cases of soul rescue I have done, that I may touch a chord deep in your soul that will trigger the remembrance of the Divine being you really are! That you may once again accept your Divinity as your heritage from the beloved Father/Mother God, and refuse to let the negativity all around the world touch you; and, instead, strive to become the "Beacon of Light" we were all meant to be.

I love you

Carole

Chapter One

THE BEGINNING OF THE PATHWAY

The soul knows when it is time for its Spiritual awakening. It can be at a young age or it can be much later down the road. For me it was when I was past forty, although, as I look back, I always felt different from others my age.

When I was sixteen years old, I worked for a summer as a nurses' aid at a general hospital in a small town called Sweetsburg (now called Cowansville), a beautiful area of the Eastern Townships in the province of Quebec, Canada. It seemed that somehow I was always the one sent to sit beside a patient whose life was drawing to an end! For me, this was a very profound experience. Somehow, I felt very close to God at these moments, knowing that this person's time on earth was ending. One day a nine month old baby died. I remember standing beside his crib and putting my hand about six inches above his chest, because I could literally sense his soul leaving the body.

As I look back now it seems strange, as I had been raised a Protestant. I remember going to church about once a year, on Easter Sunday, and there was not much "religion" taught in the schools. I had never known anyone that was a medium, or even psychic; and I had not read, nor had the desire to read, on the subject.

My Spiritual awakening really began in 1977, when I felt the need to know more about the psychic field and spirituality. This led me on my long search for knowledge, to discover what there was to man, other than the physical body. One day an advertisement on mind control courses in a Montreal newspaper caught my eye. This ad had appeared in this newspaper for years, and I had never noticed it before. I took this course and found it fascinating, but I knew there was more. I found a private school which gave courses in parapsychology, and travelled a hundred miles two nights a week for several months to attend. From this I went on to the study of hypnosis.

During those months I felt a lot of very strong energy coming into my body, especially my hands. At times it was so strong that my hands ached. This was all very strange to me, but I believed that this energy should be used for healing. My best friend Lucille and I were very compatible, and I started removing her headaches and backaches within a couple of minutes through the laying on of hands technique or by projecting healing over the telephone.

About the same period, we both became fascinated with spirit communication. We decided to try a technique resembling a homemade ouija board, using a cutout alphabet and numbers placed in a circle on a table. By placing a glass upside down, and both of us putting a finger on the bottom of the glass at the same time, it would start to move very quickly to different letters of the alphabet. As we wrote them down one by one, we soon realized that these letters formed complete sentences and then paragraphs. We were so intrigued by this that we started to hold a seance one night a week. Different members of our families, plus a couple of Spiritual guides, came through and gave us very significant messages.

At times we realized it could possibly be our subconscious minds, but at other moments we knew it had to be the spirit talking. The messages received were unknown to us, and had to be verified by the people for whom they were meant. One message still stands out in my mind. We received a message from a guide that said "the cure for cancer is in the apricot". This was back in the winter of 1978, and there was no way on God's earth we could have known this consciously or subconsciously. There was a treatment called "laetrile" that was discovered in the 1980's. Because it was not allowed on the market by the U.S. Government, people were risking prison, kidnapping their own children who were dying of cancer in hospitals, to take them to Mexico where they could be treated with this product. It was made from *apricot pits*!

The healing energy which I felt in my hands continued into the year 1978. Living in a small town, and being in partnership with my husband in a professional business, kept me from sharing with local people. I knew the stigma attached to being a healer, not to mention the strict laws prohibiting it. To be honest, I believe that living almost across from the Catholic church, and knowing that 99% of the people in the town were Catholics attending mass regularly, was a deterrent to me. I decided to keep a very low profile with this side of my life.

In July of 1978, I went to a meeting at the Spiritual Science Fellowship in Montreal. It was founded by Marilyn Zwaig Rossner, a well known medium in the city. She is now known in many parts of the world, including countries in the Eastern block, where she has worked relentlessly to share her gifts of the spirit with people from all walks of life, especially the scientific minded which are very advanced in healing with energies. They are so far ahead of America in the proof of healing using alternative methods, that I wonder if we will every catch up. Thank God that many of our young doctors coming out of medical school today have had an awakening; and they are beginning to understand that the **whole person** must be treated, not just the physical body. Until we accept the fact that for every "effect" there is a "cause", and search for the reason behind the illness, we cannot expect a permanent cure.

Marilyn is a beautiful soul that has done so much to advance the Spiritual and psychic movement in Montreal and all across Canada. There are now chapters of the fellowship in several American states and in Europe. Marilyn makes many appearances on international T.V. and radio, and gives lectures and workshops all over North America and Europe. She has a Ph.D. in child behavior and works with handicapped children, often using her intuitive gift to help them break through blockages. She has written a wonderful book called *Yoga Psychotherapy and Children*, which is being translated for European countries. No matter where she is speaking, whether it be to a group of scientists, or the wife of a head of state, she always gets across her Spiritual message of "proof of survival." Her husband John, who seconds her so beautifully in her work, is an Anglican Priest who has written books on parapsychology. These books are used in universities today. Marilyn and John make a strange little couple. As intellectual as John is, he often reminds me of an absent minded professor lost in his thoughts; Marilyn is just the opposite, very down to earth.

A week later, I called Marilyn for an appointment for a consultation. The reading consisted of her tuning into my past, present, future, and even some past lives. She told me that there were some very important writings that would be coming through me, and that I would be opening the doors to doctors in hospitals.

I went to Florida a month later for a vacation. Always on my search for more knowledge, while there I planned to visit the Arthur Ford Academy of Parapsychology in Miami. Of course, on arriving in Ft. Lauderdale, the first thing I did was rush to the Academy. Jan, one of their mediums who helped give the courses and workshops, gave me a reading. She also talked about the writing I would be doing, and the gift of healing, among many other things; and said that, in time, I would be travelling all over the world, sharing the gifts of Spirit which I had been given. She said that in thirteen months something was going to happen, and that everything was going to start to open for me then.

In January of 1979, I went back to Florida with my husband, where we planned to spend three months. I took the academy's intensive Mediumship Course, which was given by Pat and Bud Hayes, the founders of the Academy. Pat was Arthur Ford's secretary before he passed into the Spirit World, and had stayed in close contact with Arthur after his passing. She was given the techniques by him from the other side. For three days, five to ten people went to her home and lived together day and night. After the three days were over, we could sit in front of a person, take their hands for a couple of minutes to tune into their vibration, and then give them an hour long reading. During those months, I also took other courses on Spirit communication, seances, etc. For me this was really the beginning. I had finally found that for which I had been searching for three years or more! Before leaving for Canada in March, I had a second reading with Jan. She still mentioned something important happening in October, which was the thirteen month period she had seen in her reading the year before.

In September, I went back to Florida for three weeks by myself. Through a missed appointment with an astrologer, I ended up with a consultation with a Spiritual healer named Lew Smith, a lovely man with a beautiful soul. I fell in love with him on sight. He was in his seventies, and believed he was going to live until he was one hundred and twenty-four years old. He did what is called a "psychic evaluation", working with Spirit doctors and Guides. Using a pendulum, he was able to diagnose any problem in the physical body. He told me all the attitudes which were negative and had to change in order to be in harmony. He did healing and working with energies, using the techniques he had been given from the World of Spirit. Arthur Ford, a good friend of his while he was on the earth plane, and Chander Sen, a Master Guide about whom much had been written in the book *The Masters of The Far East*, were two of these souls. But the spirit that worked with him constantly for his psychic diagnosis was Dr. Edward Bach, whose last lifetime had been in England. Through his psychic and Spiritual gifts, he had discovered the "Bach Flower Remedies", which are still sold all over the world today. He passed to the other side in 1936 at the age of fifty and has been working from the Spirit World ever since.

In January 1980, my husband and I again went to Florida for the winter. The first thing I did was to let Lew know that I was there and was ready to take my intensive healing course with him. He refused most patients that week; and I lived in his home, working from morning till night, sometimes until I was exhausted. But he still had plenty of energy! His healing techniques were fascinating, and I was in seventh heaven, watching the beautiful way he could communicate with Dr. Bach, for the diagnosis of physical problems. Chander Sen did the healings for the back problems, and there were a lot of instant healings. By the end of the week, I had learned all he needed to teach me; and I left with all the books and charts necessary for me to work on my own. Although I stayed in Ft. Lauderdale until the end of February, I was anxious to get home to Canada, to practice all I had learned.

When I returned, I did what I called "Life Readings", and combined them with psychic evaluations and Spiritual counselling. I also did healing with the techniques learned; but I had to be careful, as this was against the law. I was still very much involved in our business during this period, for Jan had told me during her first reading: "It is very important that you focus into the physical business for a few years because, for some reason, your work in healing will be with people who don't believe, rather than those that do. They must be able to relate to you as a physical, material person!"

The Beginning of it All

My friend Michelyne came to me one day, and asked if I would get a group together one night a week for a course on meditation and parapsychology.

We soon found ten people who were interested in participating in this class, and I started an eight week beginners' course in all the basics of the psychic and Spiritual field. I decided to give two sessions a year, one in the Fall and one in the Spring. It was at this moment that I founded my center, which I called "The Institute of Universal and Spiritual Knowledge".

The fourth night of the beginners' course was always the class on proof of survival. At that time, I didn't have any trance mediums and was using the techniques I had learned at the Arthur Ford Academy. We formed a circle and held hands, having one student sit outside the circle. We would go into our state of altered consciousness through a certain breathing technique; and, when we were ready, the one outside the circle would call the name of someone they know, who had passed over to the spirit world, three times. This would attract the spirit to us, and we would start picking up information about this person. Even though the students had no prior experience, by having raised our vibrations and gone into our state of altered consciousness, the soul was able to reach us.

I called the information coming through "trivia", because it was more for identification than anything else. Most of it was received in picture form. I remember one student saying she was hearing church bells, and another seeing a shovel. What none of us knew was that the soul whose name was being called had spent most of his life as a caretaker of a Catholic Church. His duties included ringing the bells and digging graves. What came through was always very fascinating and evidential!

The next step consisted of having the student ask the spirit questions telepathically, and someone in the circle would receive the answer. At times they had to ask other family members, who were not present, if the answers received were exact. This was always proof to them that the answers they were getting were really coming from the spirit.

One of the students was Jacqueline, a woman in her fifties. When her turn came to sit outside the circle, two souls came through. They were her two children who had died; one a very young baby who had since grown up in the Spirit World, and the other a son who had passed in his teens. Even though she was searching for her Spiritual pathway, these revelations and proof of survival were quite a shock to her! Jacqueline's daughter also attended this class. Although her mother never shared any of her experiences with her husband, her daughter told her husband what had transpired. He forbade her to continue the course. Jacqueline was unable to finish the course, as she travelled with her daughter. **This is where start the experiences related in this book!**

Chapter Two

MY FIRST SOUL RESCUE CASE

A week later I received a call from Jacqueline, the mother who had been attending my classes. She had been having all kinds of problems with disturbances in her home and sensed a presence which gave her the shivers. She felt someone slip his hand under her pillow at night, and heard the sound of the bedroom switch being snapped on, although the light never came on. I asked her if anyone close to her had passed to spirit recently, and she said that her brother-in-law had died two weeks before. I felt that it was probably him. I told her I would come on Saturday, with some of my students, to hold a seance and try to help whoever it was to go to the Light.

At 2:00 p.m. I arrived with two of my students. One of these students, Jocelyne, had originally come to me for help. Although she had been blessed with many Spiritual gifts, she had never learned how to use them or protect herself from psychic attack. A few years before, she had had a relationship with a man who had controlled her very strongly through hypnosis techniques. Even though they were no longer together, he still had great power over her. At some point black magic was used against her by a group who were able to project all kinds of physical pain into her body. There came a time that she was such a physical, mental and emotional wreck, that people thought she was a drug addict; even though she had never taken anything stronger than an aspirin for the blinding headaches and constant pain in every area of her body. She would be working at her desk and suddenly swear words would come spewing out of her mouth, to the shock of her fellow workers.

After her first reading, she told me that if I had not believed her when she told me about the voices she had been hearing, and all she had been through, she had planned on going home and taking her own life. She could no longer stand the pain and the fact that everyone thought she was crazy. During her reading, she heard the voice of a Spirit doctor who gave his name, say: "You have finally found the person whom we promised would be put on your path to help you!" I did a healing on her, and she started my courses immediately. A few weeks later, Spirit asked that I take the time to do a complete exorcism on her, which I did with the help of one of my students. It took about an hour and a half, with the Guides helping as best they could from their side; but, in these cases, we have to do most of the work.

We started our seance at Jacqueline's house by forming a circle, holding hands, and going into our state of altered consciousness to try to pick up what we could about the spirit. Jocelyne, who had never been in a trance state before, started channeling the spirit almost immediately. He identified himself as Jacqueline's brother-in-law. He had been trying to make his presence known to let her know that all the things they talked about in the hospital during her visits were true. She had told him about the courses she was taking at my center, and talked about survival after death. He had not wanted to scare her, but had wanted to confirm the fact that life continued after the state called death. They discussed personal matters for several minutes, because there had been some misunderstandings which had caused a rift in the family, and he asked her to take the first step in bringing the family back together. At the end of the conversation, because of her fear of spirits, Jacqueline asked him to please not stay in her house. We all had a good laugh when he said, in an amused way, "Jacqueline, when I was in my physical body, I never lived in your house! Why on earth do you think I'd want to live there now?"

Because this was Jocelyne's first time in a trance state, I watched very carefully to be certain she came back very gently. But, before she did, she said, "Gary? Barry?". I knew it was another spirit, and it had to be someone one of us knew. Immediately I thought of my nephew and god-son Barry. He had lived in Vermont with his family, and had been killed in a sawmill accident about six years before at the age of twenty-two. When I asked if he were Barry, he said, "Auntie, I am here!"

Barry was a wonderful young man, and a very loving and supportive son to my sister Shirley during his short time on earth. Therefore, it was a great shock to all of the family when the accident occurred; although, with the Spiritual knowledge I have today, I know an accident does not exist. This was just a way of giving a learning experience to many people who knew and loved him. In addition, the fact that my brother Ronnie had been diagnosed with cancer a few months earlier, at the age of thirty-seven, left the family reeling.

After that first contact with me, Barry spent several years coming through to help during all my seances. There came a time when everything was done in French, however, and I guess it was time for him to go on his own evolutionary pathway on the other side.

About a week later, Jacqueline called me again. She had another problem in the house with manifestations even stronger than before! There was banging on the fridge and stove, and also on the washer and dryer in the basement. There had been no one else she knew who had passed during the week, but she worked in a hospital where several people died each week.

A young student in my advanced class, Mario, did beautiful automatic writing and was always in contact with his Guides in that way. I called and asked him to ask his Guides to tune into Jacqueline, through my vibration, and see if they could find out who the spirit was in her house. They answered immediately that the soul was very confused, but that they would try. He called back in five minutes and said the Guides gave him a first and last name of a man. I immediately called Jacqueline and asked if anyone by that name had died in the hospital during the last few days? She replied that there were usually a few deaths each day, but she would have to wait until Monday to find out, as the office was closed. When she called back, she told me that a patient by this name had died a few days before. When they told her the room number, she remembered him; but had not known his name at the time. He had been in a coma for awhile. When she was in his room cleaning, she would stand by his bed and ask that, when he got to the other side, would he please help her in making her husband more understanding of her Spiritual growth, so that he would be less grouchy and more loving. It seemed that she had been able to make him understand, but had gotten a little more than she bargained for! I was in awe of the way the Guides, working through Mario, could come up with a first and last name that was exactly right. (Mario had never met Jacqueline). I still had much to learn about the power of these wonderful Spirit Helpers!

I returned to Jacqueline's house on Sunday, although she was working until four o'clock. Jocelyne and Ginette, another advanced student who had also started to channel, came with me. We began the seance, and Dr. Bach started to come through my mediums. He said that Jacques had been there but had left. He would be back when we were gone. I knew that the only thing we could do was to wait for Jacqueline to return, because I knew he would follow her home.

When she arrived she was very upset that we hadn't "gotten rid" of him. I told her to sit down in the circle; that now we would be able to get the job done. Both of the mediums went into trance, but he didn't want to come through either one of them. Finally, the Guides "forced" him in; and, as he came through, he was crying and begging us not to make him leave! I asked him why he had followed Jacqueline home, and he answered "because she reminds me of my mother", and gave us her first name. Talking to him very gently and lovingly, I told him that he had died and was now in a new place. He could no longer stay here, but had to go on his own soul path. He still asked us to let him stay, promising that he wouldn't make any more noise, but I told him that he had to leave. Although it did not make Jacqueline happy, I told him he could come back once in awhile to visit her, to bring her encouragement and protection. Much to our amusement, she kept repeating, "If you come, don't come too often and don't stay long". She scolded her daughter for having told her that we could talk to people who were in a coma, and that they could understand and help us. Her daughter answered: "If you are stupid enough to try all the things I tell you about which I have read, that's your problem!"

Chapter Three

WORKING WITH THE SPIRIT WORLD

I continued giving my courses twice a year, always insisting that everyone start with the beginners' class, because it is imperative that we have the basics when we start opening to the psychic and spiritual realm. It is very dangerous to awaken and try to do it on our own, because this is where people get into trouble. They rush out and buy a ouija board, or try automatic writing, and, first thing they know, they open a door they don't know how to close. I have been called in on many cases where this has happened. I have had to **"clear"** the house and close off the passage, and warn them to never try anything like that again! I have referred them to someone in their area for development classes, if they wanted to continue, so that they would be taught properly.

Sometimes I am in shock when I see all the "psychics" out there today, offering a one day workshop to teach channeling to people from all walks of life. They have no idea what they are getting into! I know of someone who gave a three hour workshop to sixty-five people at one time, most of them with no prior experience in the field. I personally met one who walked out that night with his aura wide open, and experienced some very bad side effects. He could "read" everyone he met, and told them things about themselves. He shouldn't have had knowledge of them, and found himself in a lot of trouble. Ending up with a nervous breakdown, he lost his job as a pilot. His life was constantly out of balance, and many times he was on the verge of suicide. Thank God he finally met a good friend of mine, a wonderful medium, who helped him straighten out his life by learning to balance himself and keep his aura closed.

When we start playing around with the fourth dimension, **"like attracts like"**. This means that if we are not awakened to the spiritual side of our nature, we attract to us only the souls in the lower astral. These beings are still in the lowest state of mind, having refused to move to a higher dimension. They prefer staying close to the earth, trying to influence those still on a very low vibratory rate because of their refusal to accept the spiritual side of their being.

This is the reason for many of the obsession and possession cases which have been documented. As we move down the road, with more and more people taking drugs and alcohol because of their need to run away from life, we shall see many more looking for help. The use of these two "destroyers of life" causes a crack in the aura, and permits those in the lower astral plane to reach us very easily by influencing us with their negative way of thinking.

One day Bernard, a young man who had tried to commit suicide, came to me for help. We talked several times, and he started my course right away. He had some beautiful spiritual gifts, the strongest being the potential to be a deep trance medium. His mother Maria, brother Mario, cousin Robert, and Robert's wife Ginette all joined him in the development class and advanced courses thereafter. Bernard and Ginette were deep trance mediums, and Maria was a beautiful mental medium. She received all her information in her mind, and wrote it down one phrase at a time. Mario did automatic writing, and was constantly in contact with his guides in this manner. Robert had one of the most spiritual vibrations I have ever seen. The first time I met him, I felt his aura about eight feet from him. He had a very strong healing gift.

Now that I had three trance mediums in my advanced class, spirit started to bring us more and more soul rescue cases. The guides always came through first, and gave us Spiritual teachings. As we progressed, they started bringing through many children who had been murdered, to be put into the Light. Sometimes they would give us a first name; but, at one point, one of them told us that the Nun helping them advised them to not give their real names or too many details. She said we would want to investigate, and this was not the goal of the soul rescue work for the time being.

Several little girls came back through a medium in trance shortly after having been put over into the Light, and started giving more details about their murder. They explained they had been cut into pieces and buried. There had been three or four young girls from within a forty mile radius of Montreal who had disappeared within a couple of years, and had never been found. From some of the details we had been given, we felt they had lived in our region. One of the girls told us where she had been buried; and one of the students, along with two friends, decided to go to the area and do some digging. It was in a spot where there were a few trees, but very close to the highway where the Provincial Police patrolled constantly. They pulled off the road, and raised the hood of their car in case the police stopped. They planned to say that the motor had overheated, and they were letting it cool. The spirit of the girl directed them through Mario and his automatic writing. When they had dug down about a foot, they found a man's leather glove encrusted with dirt and what looked like blood stains. They put the glove aside to bring back to me; and, as expected, the police arrived. They had to stop and never went back. I was shocked that they had taken such a chance. Imagine what the police would have said if they had found the body! Who would have believed that the information came from the Spirit World, and not from someone who had firsthand knowledge of the circumstances of the murder?

They brought the glove back to me, to see what I could get from the vibrations. As I touched it, I felt sick to my stomach. It felt as if I were touching something very evil, and I started to shake. I told them never to go back there again! The Spirit World told the family that someone would be sent later on to help the police bring these sick individuals who murdered children to justice. A soul who had been an R.C.M.P. officer was looking forward to working with them when the time was right; but, for now, they had more important things to do. During that seance, the spirit that talked to us gave us much information about the killer; his nickname in the bike gang to which he belonged, the area of Montreal where he lived, the three earrings he wore in one ear, and his Harley Davidson Motorcycle which they told us was registered in someone else's name. They said that if he were not caught soon, he would kill again! **I would have reason to remember those words later on!**

Our weekly classes advanced, with all of the students developing their spiritual gifts of clairvoyance, Spiritual healing and mediumship. When a person is drawn to the psychic and spiritual field, it is usually because of an awakening of the soul; and someone is put on their path to help them understand. The soul only awakens when the time is right, usually the moment they have chosen before incarnating on earth. Each person has free will, and I let them grow at their own pace. Because Spiritual gifts unfold, and should not be forced, I teach natural, spiritual and karmic law, helping them put everything in their own lives in perspective.

When we start the awakening and want to advance, we often have problems at home and in other areas of our lives. Those around us don't understand where we are "coming from", we have trouble understanding the changes ourselves. We must find people "of a like mind", which usually means letting go of old friends and making new ones who are on the same spiritual path.

Christ had always been very important in my life. Almost like an inner knowledge that I had known him at some point in time. I began to feel the desire to have a life size painting of him, to hang on the wall in my Spiritual center. My friend Michelyne had started taking painting lessons, and I asked her to paint the portrait for me. I proudly hung it on my wall when it was ready, and would sit the people who came to me for Spiritual healing on a stool in front of it. Our seances were always held in a circle in the same room, and I knew we were well protected.

Edward Bach, my Spirit Doctor, worked with me for psychic diagnosis through the use of a pendulum. He started coming through my mediums, and would verbally give me his diagnosis of some of my cases when I asked him to do so. His loving energy and dry sense of humor were greatly appreciated by all. We also had Master Guides channeling each night, teaching us the Spirituality needed to put to use in our everyday lives.

One night a guide came through and asked for permission to put a psychic door in my home, for the lost souls to go through. He told me to put it anywhere I wished, and they would put a very strong beam of light over the house to direct them to it. They said it would be a little bothersome for me, as I would hear the crackings, and sometimes the sound of footsteps, as the spirits came in. I would be able to sense their presence. It had only been tried twice before in the history of humanity, and one experience had failed. I felt very blessed to have been given the opportunity to serve in this way.

I decided to put the door in my living room, but I really didn't feel comfortable with it there. With the television, and friends coming in and out, there was just too much happening. In our next course, after we had said our opening prayer and Ginette had gone into a trance, a guide came through and asked to be left alone in the room. A little surprised because this was the first time anything like this had happened, I said "Of course. May I leave the recorder on?" He agreed. There were about a dozen students, and we all got up and went out into the hall. I heard him start to talk out loud: "Beloved Father, come down on this house...", and I quietly closed the door. We were all very quiet, mystified over what was happening. After about five minutes, he clapped his hands to let us know we could return. As we filed in and took our places, he looked around at everyone and said: **"My Father has decided that the door will be where my picture is!"**

We continued our class. Another guide came in, giving personal messages, mostly regarding each student's Spiritual growth. The batteries in my recorder lasted about twenty minutes that night instead of the usual three hours, so I knew that a very powerful energy had been in the room. After everyone left, I was very anxious to listen to the tape. It said, *"Beloved Father, come down! Come down on this house of Light and Love, where so many people find peace and healing! Put Your loving vibrations in this place, so that everyone who enters may feel Your presence."* He invoked God once again in about the same words, as if to reinforce the energy. There was a pause on the tape for a couple of minutes, while he seemed to be listening to someone answering. Then he started again. *"Yes, I will tell them... I will give them your message. I shall tell them that you love them! Oh Father, I thank you for coming tonight, for having put your Light so strongly around this place, where so many souls will be able to find it."*

At first, when the lost souls started to come in, there was always a dry cracking noise in the room. Anyone who was attentive to this just knew that it was not the ordinary sound of the walls, floor, or ceiling of the home cracking. In the beginning, I was conscious of many Loving Beings in the other dimension directing the spirits to the Light. After a few days, they seemed to come in on their own, drawn to the Light over my home. They came looking for someone to help them. When I was in my bedroom at night, I would just tune in to the spot in the room where I sensed they were standing, send them love and say, "Welcome dear soul! I know you are looking for the door; so if you will just follow this Light, it will take you to the place you are looking for." In my mind, I would trace a path of light for them down to my center, which was an apartment connected to my house through a separate passageway. Some nights, several would come in; and I would feel them standing by my bed waiting for directions. If I had not closed off my energy field properly, I would sometimes feel the symptoms they had in the physical body before passing over. I always spoke to them with great love, as I sent them down to the door, feeling so blessed to be able to help in this way.

The five members of the "family group", as I called them, were advancing very well in the class. They started doing seances in their mother's home in the little town where they all lived. They would come to my course one night a week; and, occasionally, I would join them in their home.

The week after the place was chosen for the psychic door, I joined them in a seance. Doctor Edward Bach came through, and we discussed a few subjects. He told me that they had rushed to put the door in my center, because they would be bringing the boys from the Falkland War through it. This war had ended a few weeks before, after a very brief period of fighting; but many young soldiers had died in battle. They would start directing them through the door in about three weeks. He said, "It is very sad, because they were so young and didn't expect to die. It was a great shock to them. Some of them were so badly injured that it was impossible for their physical bodies to continue to function. But they still held on, and we had to cut the silver cord and take them back."

Five nights later, while I was sitting alone in my living room, I heard a dry cracking sound. This meant that a spirit had come in. As I tuned in to the spot where I heard the noise, I saw a beautiful little three year old girl with blonde hair down to her shoulders, wearing a red nightgown. She came and stood beside my chair, looking at me in a questioning way. I knew someone from the Spirit World had brought her to me for help, so I took her little astral hand in mine and said, "Come on, sweetheart, we're going to find you some little children to play with." I walked with her down the hallway to my center, placed a chair in front of my painting of Jesus, and sat down. She stood in front of me, and I could literally feel her leaning her back against my knees. As I looked at the psychic door, I could see small children in the doorway, beckoning to her with toys in their hands. I said, "These are little friends for you, and they want you to go and play with them. Would you like that?" She nodded, and moved forward into the door.

I was still sitting there when I heard a cracking sound behind me to my right! Because I was in my state of altered consciousness, without turning around I saw a young man dressed in leather pants and jacket. He held a helmet under his right arm. I psychically "knew" that his name was Jacques, he was sixteen years old, he came from Riviere-du-Loup in northern Quebec, and he had been killed in an accident while on his motorcycle. I welcomed him, and asked him to go through the door! To my left I saw a woman in her fifties, who walked with a limp because her left leg was shorter than her right. She also went through immediately! I moved my chair back to get ready to leave, when suddenly I was startled. Two young soldiers carrying a stretcher with a young man on it almost ran over me. They came from the back of the room and ran right through the Spiritual door, oblivious to my presence! I was almost in shock, and thought, "My God! It's really happening! The boys from the Falkland War have started to arrive already!" I could only send a loving prayer after them.

A few months later, Irene Griffey came to spend a week with me, as she did twice yearly. Irene was a wonderful transfiguration medium, and we had become good friends over the years. She would hold a seance every second night for my students and friends who wished to participate. She would prove survival, by the forming of the face of the spirit coming through her over her own face. It was so clear that the spirit was easily recognizable. This was done through the use of ectoplasm, a substance which is intangible and invisible; but, through the help of spirit operators, who are specialists in this field, it can become tangible and visible. This is in the category of "physical phenomena", and has been known to be used for this kind of mediumship for over a hundred years. With the raising of the vibratory rate on the planet over the past few years, Spirit now works differently with us. It uses the "electromagnetic force field" of the rare individual who has the potential to do this kind of mediumship, and all phenomena can be done in broad daylight.

We prepared the room by temporarily putting up drapes over the windows, so that the room was in complete darkness. A lamp with a small red bulb would be set on a stool in front of Irene's chair, so that her face was the only thing visible in the room when we turned the lights off. If I were to go to my center for some reason during the day, I could feel a large pile of ectoplasm being built up at the left of her chair. The Spirit World was hard at work preparing the seance for the evening.

Irene was still developing her spiritual gift of transfiguration when she first started to come to me in 1982, and could only produce faces for about seven or eight people. She was holding seances for small groups at that time in her life, and everyone got one or two faces. I usually had about twenty people who were sitting three rows deep, and I wondered how we would know who the faces were for. I asked if it would be possible to have each one draw a number, which only they would know, and Spirit would work with that. Of course the Spirit World, knowing of our plans ahead of time, said they would try this method.

Irene would sit in her chair on a slightly raised platform in the front of the room, and quickly put herself into the trance state necessary for the work. A Spiritual guide always came in to welcome us, and to give a short talk on Spirituality. He explained the natural and spiritual laws which governed the planet, and how we were subject to their control by cause and effect. Parkinson, a Spirit who was Irene's control during all the years of this work, would come in next. He would explain how the evening would proceed, as there were always a lot of people who had never attended a seance before. They were very nervous, and did not know what to expect. As Spirit worked strongly on voice vibration, the person would answer by giving his first name when his number was called. It was very important to keep the vibrations very high in the room, so that the faces would continue to build up strongly. We all welcomed each soul coming through, with a lot of love and laughter, because the joy kept the energy in the room high, and the faces were much clearer. It was wonderful to see how happy these souls were; to finally make contact with family members and let them know that they were *alive and well.* There were many tears and unblockings among those in the room. When someone leaves the physical body very quickly, we don't always have the time to say good-bye or I'm sorry. Many things are left unsaid, which leaves the one left behind with a sense of guilt weighing heavily on his heart. This was the chance to unburden themselves, and find peace in their hearts for the first time since the passing of their loved ones. The soul coming through, having evolved to a certain degree on the other side, usually explained with a great deal of love that there was no need to feel badly. It had all been a growing lesson for each of them, and to get on with their lives.

For many of my students, it was their first opportunity to meet, and physically see, one of the guides working closely with them. They always came in with a lot of love, explained some things about their spiritual pathway, and answered a question or two. Many recognized them from having seen them psychically during their meditation, or having had a picture of them drawn by a psychic artist. The guides were always received with great joy!

One of my guides is a North American Indian named Strong Bow, and we have walked together in many life-times. My strong feelings of a connection with the Native

Americans since I was a small girl, surely stems from some of these lifetimes; at least one in which he was my father. He has worked with me during my readings, often ending with a healing and balancing of the body of my client. Taking me into a light trance state, he starts the healing by standing behind the person. Always working in the etheric body, Strong Bow ends by kneeling down in front of him or her, taking both his hands, and "siphoning" off all the things that should not be in the body. I am aware of what is happening, and feel all the things being removed – pain, stress, heartbreak, etc. – in the same areas of my own body. This only lasts for a couple of minutes before it is released, for the guides never let me retain anything in my physical body that does not belong to me. I believe any pain I feel is a blessing to me for being able to do this work.

When Strong Bow worked with me for healing, he always transfigured my face so strongly that my clients could see him very clearly. He had the typical Indian face, with very high cheekbones and wrinkles, especially around his small mouth. In his words, he was in the prime of his life.

Cynthia Bradshaw, a friend I met in England while studying there in 1983 and 1984, has her own center in Camberley, Surrey. She would invite Coral Polge, one of the best psychic artists in Europe, to come to her center each year to draw psychic portraits for her students. I asked Cynthia to ask Coral to do a psychic portrait for me through the vibrations of one of my letters. I did not ask for anyone in particular, as Coral often drew pictures of family members; but, I was very happy to receive one of a beautiful Indian with a headdress. In the corner she had written "Strong Bow". It was perfect, right down to the name, and was the same face which had been coming through Irene for a few years. Now when a client describes the face he sees transfigured over mine during a healing, I laughingly tell them to turn around and look at the framed picture hanging on the wall. Immediately they identify it as the face they have seen.

There is a very strong love bond between Strong Bow and me, for I know he is always there for me! Whenever I am discouraged and feeling down, I only have to think of him and immediately I feel the love flowing to me. I see the beautiful color vibration on which he works, a mixture of purple and pink, with gold threads running through it; and I feel him giving me strength to pick myself up once again. Whether I am meditating at home, or channeling elsewhere, he is always the first one through. He is also my protector, as he has been since my coming to the planet.

On several occasions, people who came to my center proved that the door really did exist. They did not know that the painting of Christ with the beautiful eyes was really a doorway for the lost souls. Irene was with me when Eva Illes, a psychic artist originally from Montreal, now living in Toronto, came on a Saturday to do a day of psychic portraits for my students. When Irene was there, I always took my painting off the wall and put it in a large closet that was in the other half of my center. I did not want it damaged by the third row of chairs lined up against the wall for Irene's people.

Eva was to use the other half of the center, which was designed like a double living room which could be closed off with sliding glass doors. She set up her easel and placed her chair in front of it, ready for a day of work. Her back was to the closet, which was closed. She knew nothing about the painting, or that I had put it in the closet three days before.

The students were scheduled for every half hour, and I would usually be around to translate for those who didn't speak English. Eva was Hungarian, and only spoke a few words of French. She is always in a light trance state while doing her drawings, and her face transfigures during that time. Being in an altered state, she was naturally conscious of what was happening around her in the other dimensions. After finishing a few of the charcoal paintings of guides, she called out to me: "Carole, I don't know what is happening, but the spirits walk past me one after the other, and they go into the closet. I don't know where they go, but they don't come back! They don't speak to me or bother me, and I don't know who they are; but they parade by one after the other, and they don't come back!"

I always laugh when I think of this; because I can still hear Eva, with her strong Hungarian accent, almost in shock. It was a wonderful surprise for me. When I put the painting in the closet for a few days, I assumed that the spirits would go through the wall in the usual place. I now had my proof that the painting was really the door to the Spirit World for the lost souls, just as I had been told by the Spirit Guides; although I never really doubted it for a moment.

We had confirmation again when Bernard was coming out of his deep trance state after an evening of channelling. I always watch my mediums closely to see that they come back very gently. Suddenly, I realized that another spirit was in his body, ready to come through. As he came in, he was a bit aggressive and said, "If that fat guy thinks I'm not coming through, he's crazy! I've been sitting on that sofa for a week, and I'm not waiting any longer!" So I laughed and welcomed him, and we started to talk. I said something about his going to the Light, and he replied that he knew he was dead. I said fine, now we can understand each other. He said, "I want to ask you something. What's that door over there?", and he pointed to the painting. I answered that it was the door to Heaven. He said: "Heaven, Heaven! You can't tell me that what I'm living is Hell! During the time I've been sitting on the sofa waiting for tonight, all those people walked past me and went in there; and not a damn one came out!" I asked if he would like to go and see for himself, and he jerked back and said, "No way! There must be some kind of a siphon that sucks them in, and they can't get back out. I'm not going near it!" I told him he couldn't be happy roaming around with nowhere to call "home", and he replied "I'm fine, I go all over the place. I see the trees and flowers and all kinds of things; and I'm not bored. When my wife passed, I thought she would stop and talk to me, but she just went over like that!", and he snapped his fingers. He bent towards me and whispered, "I guess she was afraid that I would talk to her about the boyfriend she had; but I didn't care. I was dead anyway!" Bernard always sat beside me across from the painting, so the spirit was facing the psychic door. We sat and chatted for a few minutes. Suddenly he pointed to the door and said, "Look, my wife is standing in the door, and she is beckoning to me. She has a cup in her hand, and says for me to come on, that my coffee is ready!" I replied, "Wonderful! She couldn't have disliked you that much, if she's coming to get you. Does she remember how you like your coffee?" He said, "Oh, yes, one cream and two sugar. I guess I'll go with her now, and I want to thank you for your help. Tell the fat guy I'm sorry I forced my way in and shook him up, but I wasn't waiting on that sofa any longer!", and off he went. When Bernard came out of trance, he remembered getting ready to come back and mentally arguing with someone who insisted that he was coming through.

Each case was unique and sad in its own way. Many of these souls were touching the earth plane one last time.

Through the loan of a physical body, we were permitting the soul to release the trauma of its passing. Even though I usually did not tell them that they had died, but sent them into the Spirit World for the help they needed, I put a lot of love into my work. I wanted them to have the memory of someone who cared during those last moments.

Chapter Four

THE SOUL RESCUE OF MONIQUE

In January 1982, I came home from a vacation in Barbados. My husband asked me if I remembered reading a newspaper story in November about a young woman who had committed suicide by throwing herself and her three month old son into the Riviere-des-Prairies, a river in Montreal. The baby's body was found the next day, but the mother was still missing. He then told me that she was the wife of a representative of one of the insurance companies with which we had been doing business. I knew her husband Luc well, for he had been coming to our office once a month for several years. Apart from knowing he was married, I knew little about him.

Luc knew that I had something to do with parapsychology, so he called and asked to see me. He came a few days later, bringing the ten page letter his wife had left for him the morning she put the baby in his stroller and headed for the river.

Touching the letter to feel her vibration, I instantly knew that she was earthbound. I could feel her anguish, and hear her sobbing. Luc asked me when she had made her decision to end her life. I tuned into the last day, and saw her very depressed. Sitting on her sofa in a pink housecoat, she was writing the letter to Luc and crying at the same time. When she was finished, she dressed herself and the baby, put him in his stroller and left the house. She walked about a mile, and dropped the baby into the water behind a school. I knew that she had thrown herself in fifty or one hundred feet further down the river. Luc confirmed that the color pink was prominent in her housecoat.

Monique had been very depressed since the baby's birth, and was being treated by the doctor who had performed the delivery. Many women suffer from "post partum depression", but he hadn't realized to what extent. Her pregnancy progressed without problems, and she insisted on working until the last month. Maybe this, along with the fact that she was having her first baby at thirty-five years old, was just too much for her; she just couldn't seem to get it all together! The house would be untouched when Luc came home at night, so he would pitch in and do the dishes, washing and cleaning. Seeing him do this made her feel even more inadequate. It just seemed to become a vicious circle, and she could see no other solution. I told him my class would be holding a seance with a medium in trance in a few days, and we would try to bring her through and convince her to go to the Light.

On the night of the seance, Jocelyne went into the trance state and I called in Monique. I knew she had followed Luc to my house the week before, so it wouldn't be hard. She controlled Jocelyne almost immediately, and asked who we were and what we wanted. I informed her that something had happened, and she was to go to the Light in the center of the circle. She argued that she wasn't going anywhere, and was staying in her home. Finally, I told her very gently that she could no longer stay in her home; because she had died. She started to sob, and said, "Me, dead? No! No!,

God in Heaven, it's not possible! I only want to be in my home!" Immediately, she left Jocelyne's body.

I called Luc the next day to tell him what had happened. He said that the phrase "God in Heaven" was one she used very often while in the physical body. I knew that we would have to go to the house to do the soul rescue, or she would not leave. Luc had felt Monique's presence in his home often, and the cat would run down the hall chasing an invisible ball. Other times, he would stand on his hind legs at Monique's side of the bed, twirling a paw in mid air. It were as if someone had extended an invisible finger for him so that he could play.

On the 12th of February, I made arrangements to go to Luc's apartment with Jocelyne as the medium. Linda, one of my young students with a beautiful gift of healing, came as well. She always came with me when I did soul rescue work.

We walked into the house and began to go from room to room to discern. As we walked back into the living room, Jocelyne felt herself being pushed from behind. I knew this was Monique trying to push her out of the house, for Luc said she had been extremely jealous. Not realizing that she had made the transition, she did not want Luc bringing a pretty young woman she did not know into her home. Jocelyne sat with her back to the wall, and I set up my tape recorder. Luc sat on the sofa partly facing her.

She came in within a couple of minutes; in a very emotional state, and I had to gently calm her down.

Monique
  – WHAT ARE YOU DOING HERE?
Carole
  – We want to help you, Monique.

Monique
  —BUT IT'S MY HOUSE.

Carole
  — Yes, it's your house; but we have come to help you.
  Where are you, Monique, do you know?

Monique
  —I'M COLD, BUT I FEEL ALRIGHT!

Carole
  — Can you tell us more?

Monique
  —THE BABY! THE BABY!

Carole
  — Where is the baby, Monique?

Monique
  —HE'S NOT WITH ME. (Becomes agitated.)

Carole
  — It's alright, the baby is fine. Don't worry about him.

Monique
  —I WANT MY BABY.

Carole
  — You'll have your baby, don't worry. Luc will take care
  of the baby.

Monique
  —DID I DO SOMETHING?

Carole
  — Yes, you did something; but it will be alright.

Monique
  —WHERE AM I? WHERE AM I?

Carole
  — You have gone far away...you must leave the house.

Monique
— But it's my house!

Carole
— Yes, it's your house; but you are no longer at the house. You have to continue towards the Light. Do you see the Light?

Monique
— No!

Carole
— Search for the Light. You will see people who will help you.

Monique
— In my head there are all kinds of ideas!

Carole
— What sort of ideas?

Monique
— The baby.

Carole
— The baby is fine! Can you tell me what is happening in your head? (She makes a rocking movement with her arms crossed in front of her.)

Monique
— I'm rocking my baby.

Carole
— Besides that, what's happening in your head?

Monique
— It's confused.

Carole
— Yes, there's a lot of confusion. Can you try to clarify it for me.

Monique
- THE BABY! IT'S TOO MUCH! I CAN'T DO EVERY-
THING. THE PILLS MADE MY HEAD FEEL STRANGE!
Carole
- What kind of pills did you take?
MONIQUE
- IT FEELS LIKE I FORGET EVERYTHING. I CAN'T GET
ANYTHING DONE; I CAN'T DO ANYTHING RIGHT.
Carole
- Everything will be fine.
Monique
- OTHERS SEEM TO BE ABLE TO DO IT, BUT I JUST
CAN'T SEEM TO GET IT ALL TOGETHER.
Carole
- You'll get it together. You're a wonderful woman,
Monique.
Monique
- MY HEAD! IT'S WORSE THAN USUAL! ALL THE CON-
FUSION IN MY HEAD, THE BABY CRYING; I MADE MY
DECISION!
Carole
- What did you decide?
Monique
- I CAN'T GO ON THIS WAY! I FEEL REMOTE FROM
EVERYTHING; I DON'T FEEL THE SAME AS USUAL. I
CAN NEVER GET ANYTHING DONE, EVERYTHING SEEMS
SLOW. I WANT TO GO FAST AND IT DOESN'T WORK.
I'M SICK AT TIMES.
Carole
- What did you decide to do?
Monique
- I TOOK SOME PILLS.

Carole
   — How many?

Monique
   — I DON'T KNOW. IT HAD AN EFFECT. I FELT BETTER;
   I FELT CALMER.

At this moment Luc needed some answers of his own
and started to ask her a few questions:

Luc
   — Where did you get the pills, Monique?

Monique
   — IN THE MEDICINE CABINET.

Luc
   — All that you had to take from there were vitamins.

Monique
   — YES, BUT SOMETIMES...

Luc
   — Sometimes you got into something else?

Monique
   — SOMETIMES...

Luc
   — Where is the bottle? Were they nerve pills?

Monique
   — NERVES.

Luc
   — There are no nerve pills here.

Monique
   — SOMETIMES WE CAN GO AND BUY SOME.

Luc
   — Without a prescription?

Monique
- DON'T NEED A PRESCRIPTION FOR THOSE; I'VE TAKEN
THEM BEFORE.

Luc
- At which drugstore did you buy them?

Monique
- I CAN'T REMEMBER! BUT HE SAID IT WASN'T IMPOR-
TANT. HE SAID THAT IT HAPPENED THAT WOMEN
GOT DISCOURAGED SOMETIMES; THAT IT WOULD PASS.
(She was either talking about the doctor or the pharma-
cist.)

Luc
- Why didn't you talk to me about it? You know I always
helped you when I could.

Monique
- I FELT I WAS A BURDEN.

Luc
- You know very well that I loved you, and I still love you.
Why didn't you tell me or call me at the office? You
know I would have come right away.

Monique
- YES, I KNOW ALL THAT; BUT I WAS LIKE A CHILD.
I DIDN'T FEEL LIKE A WOMAN.

Luc
- Yes, you were a woman, Monique. Why didn't you go
upstairs to my mother's with the baby?

Monique
- No! I WANTED HIM JUST FOR MYSELF. BUT SOME-
TIMES I FELT HE TOOK UP TOO MUCH SPACE.

Luc
- We had discussed the fact that it would be hard with a
baby. I told you there would be highs and lows, as we

had been living selfishly for twelve years. You wanted
the baby, and so did I.

Monique

   — Yes, I know all that, but I didn't think it
   would be this way! I couldn't imagine it being
   this hard. The other women didn't say that
   it would be like this!

Luc

   — It's not always easy with a baby!

Monique

   — No, but he cried! He cried all the time!

The discussion between Luc and Monique went on for
several more minutes. When a tragedy like this happens in
the life of a young couple, the one who is left always has
a sense of guilt and wonders where he or she went wrong.
At one point he asked her a question and she had difficulty
answering. My nephew Barry, who was one of the controls
from the Spirit World that night, came through and said to
let her tell us only what she could. She was very confused,
and might not be able to remember some names and all the
details. Also, she didn't realize what she had done, so we
had to be very careful not to traumatize her more than she
already was.

Monique

   — But what are they doing here?

Carole

   — We came to help you, Monique. Do you remember what
   happened?

Monique

   — I said, "I can't go on like this. I love Luc so

MUCH, AND THE BABY TOO; SOMETIMES TOO MUCH...I
AM HAPPY, I WANTED HIM, BUT I COULDN'T FACE
EVERYTHING. I THOUGHT ABOUT IT FOR A LONG
TIME!

Luc

– Thought about what?

Monique

– THIS DECISION TO END IT ALL.

Luc

– You weren't happy with me?

Monique

– YES, I WAS VERY HAPPY.

Carole

– What happened that morning?

Monique

– I GOT UP... I DID SOME THINGS AROUND THE HOUSE...
I FELT AS IF I COULDN'T GET ANYTHING DONE. I SAT
DOWN ON THE SOFA... AND AFTER I...

Luc

– Did you take some pills or something?

Monique

– YES, AND IT DIDN'T GET ANY BETTER. IN MY HEAD
EVERYTHING STARTED AGAIN. I SAID TO MYSELF,
"LUC IS GOING TO GET TIRED OF IT ALL. HE'S VERY
PATIENT, HE'S VERY CALM, BUT FOR ME IT'S WORSE
THAN EVER!" I WANTED THE BABY JUST FOR MY-
SELF. I THOUGHT, "I'LL HAVE TO END IT ALL AS
SOON AS POSSIBLE!" I WROTE... I CRIED... I WANTED
TO TAKE A WALK. IT WAS LIKE AN OBSESSION IN MY
MIND. AT CERTAIN TIMES IT WAS LIKE AN OBSESSION
TO END IT ALL. IT WOULD COME... AND IT WOULD

GO; THEN IT WOULD COME BACK AGAIN. WHEN LUC
WAS HERE, IT WASN'T AS BAD. I WANTED TO TELL
HIM, BUT I FELT THAT IT WAS STUPID. I DRESSED
THE BABY...

Carole
– What is the baby's name?

Here Barry came in again, and said, "She has difficulty
remembering. She doesn't know about the baby, (having
blocked it out because it was too painful), so it's better not
to mention him. She will give you some information, but
maybe not what you want to know. It hasn't been very long,
and she is too confused."

Monique
– LUC, LUC, AM I AT HOME? HAS SHE TAKEN MY
PLACE?

Luc
– They want to help you, and you know I always wanted
to help you.

Monique
– THE BABY! HE'S NOT HERE! I'M IN OUR BEDROOM.
(She had suddenly projected herself into their bedroom
where the crib was.)

Luc
– The baby is a little angel.

Monique
– (Turning to me) IS IT TRUE?

Carole
– Yes.

Monique
– WHY?

Carole

– He was sick. God came and got him. (She then let out
a great sigh of relief.)

Monique

– I WAS AFRAID! I DIDN'T DO ANYTHING THAT...?

She had started to remember what had happened and
began to cry.

Monique

– I WANTED TO GET HIM BACK... I WANTED TO, BUT
HE SLIPPED FROM MY HANDS. I WANTED TO DO IT,
AND THEN I DIDN'T WANT TO ANYMORE. BUT I
COULDN'T REACH HIM.

Carole

– You changed your mind?

Monique

– YES, BUT IT WAS TOO LATE!

Carole

– Don't worry, he is fine.

Monique

– (Still sobbing) I SANK! I SANK! I TRIED WITH MY
HANDS TO COME BACK UP! I SEARCHED WITH MY
HANDS, I WANTED TO COME BACK, BUT I COULDN'T
COME BACK.

Carole

– You have to go towards the Light now Monique. Do you
know where you are?

Monique

– YES; I'M IN THE WATER.

Carole

– Your physical body is in the water, but your spirit is no
longer in the water. You are on the other side now; you
must accept that you are no longer on the earth plane.

Monique
- I WANT TO BE AT HOME.

Luc
- To please me, Monique, you must do as we ask.

Monique
- LATER.

Luc
- You have to do it tonight! Remember I promised you I would never abandon you. You see me crying sometimes at night?

Monique
- YES, AND I DON'T WANT YOU TO CRY ANYMORE.

Luc
- Well, if you don't want me to cry anymore, you must do as we ask. Will you do it?

Carole
- Now you know that you are no longer on earth, Monique.

Monique
- THEY WILL FIND ME.

Luc
- Yes, we will find you! I'm anxious to find you, sweetheart.

Monique
- I WON'T BE PRETTY!

Luc
- I'll love you anyway.

Carole
- But you are no longer in that physical body. You are on the other side, with God.

Monique
- I NEED SO MUCH LOVE!

Luc
- I gave you a lot of love.

Monique
- IT'S DIFFERENT.

Carole
- You're going to look towards the Light. Look upwards, Monique. You will see the Light. There you will have much love. There are people there who are holding out their hands to help. Do you recognize anyone?

Monique
- I'M BEGINNING TO SEE THE LIGHT.

Carole
- Do you see the people around this Light?

Luc
- Do you see my father? Or your grandfather? Your grandmother, or Aunt Cecile?

Monique
- FIRST I WANT TO BE AT HOME.

Carole
- You can't be at home.

Monique
- I WANT TO GO AROUND AND VISIT EACH ROOM IN THE HOUSE.

Carole
- We love you, Monique. We want to help you.

Monique
- I THOUGHT YOU WERE HERE TO TAKE MY PLACE.

Carole
- No, we didn't come to take your place; we only came to help you.

Monique

> – LUC, YOU HAVE TO LIVE DIFFERENTLY. YOU HAVE TO LOVE ME, BUT IN A DIFFERENT WAY. I AM NO LONGER THERE.

Luc

> – You will always be in my heart!

Monique

> – YOU MUST FORGET ME; LIVE YOUR LIFE AND BE HAPPY. WE MUST TALK ABOUT THE PRESENT. I MUST LEAVE, AND I WANT TO TELL YOU THAT YOU MUST TAKE YOURSELF IN HAND. YOU HAD ABSOLUTELY NO RESPONSIBILITY IN ALL OF THIS; I ALONE MADE THE DECISION. I WANTED TO DRAW BACK, BUT IT WAS TOO LATE. YOU MUST START A NEW LIFE. I LOVE YOU AND I HAVE ALWAYS LOVED YOU. I NOW ACCEPT TO FOLLOW YOUR LIGHT, MADAME, ON THE CONDITION THAT I CAN LOVE AND PROTECT HIM.

Luc

> – That is what I want.

Monique

> – BUT YOU MUST ACCEPT MY DECISIONS!

Luc

> – I accept them, but it's very hard.

Monique

> – I ALONE MADE THE DECISIONS; I DO NOT WANT YOU TO FEEL ANY RESPONSIBILITY. AND ALSO TO TELL YOU THAT I LOVED YOU TOO MUCH. THANK YOU FOR ALL THAT YOU GAVE ME. THANK YOU FOR ALL THAT YOU SHARED WITH ME. I AM HAPPY TO ADVANCE INTO THE LIGHT. PLEASE PRAY FOR ME!

Carole

> – Yes, we will pray for you, Monique.

Monique
- ALSO THANK THE DIVINE PROVIDENCE FOR PUTTING THESE PEOPLE ON YOUR PATH, BECAUSE THEY MUST HELP ME TAKE THE STEP THROUGH THE NEXT STAGE; AND I THANK THEM. CONTINUE TO SURROUND ME WITH LOVE, BECAUSE I NEEDED SO MUCH. EVEN IF I RECEIVED IT, IT WAS NEVER ENOUGH. SURROUND ME WITH LOVE TO HELP ME WALK.

Luc
- Do you remember that I had talked to you about this lady? (Carole)

Monique
- YES, AND I THANK HER, BECAUSE I MUST ACCEPT! I MUST ACCEPT MY NEW LIFE AND I AM HAPPY TO BE ABLE TO FINALLY SAY THIS. ALSO, LATER ON I WILL HELP YOU; BUT FOR MANY MONTHS I WILL NOT BE THERE. BEFORE LEAVING, LUC, I MUST TELL YOU THAT YOU MUST STOP TORTURING YOURSELF ABOUT MY REASONS.

Luc
- You know that I have always had a hard head too, and I wanted to know why.

Monique
- MY HEAD STILL HURTS, BUT I KNOW THAT I WILL NO LONGER SUFFER. ALL MY IDEAS WILL BE STRAIGHT, AND MY BABY WILL BE WAITING FOR ME. HE WILL BE THE ONE TO HELP ME FIND MY PATH ONCE AGAIN. DO NOT TORTURE YOURSELF ANY LONGER WITH IT ALL. I ALONE CARRY THE RESPONSIBILITY. I ASK YOU TO BE STRONG, TO CONTINUE YOUR WORK AND YOUR AMBITIONS. EACH DAY, HELP ME TO WALK IN THIS LIGHT, WHICH IS FOR ME ANOTHER STAGE.

Luc

– Yes, I will help you.

Monique

– IT IS WITH ALL MY LOVE THAT I ASK THAT YOU START A NEW LIFE, TO GIVE YOURSELF SOME HAPPINESS EVERYDAY, AND ALSO SOME REST. DON'T CRY ANYMORE! IT HURT ME SO MUCH TO SEE YOU CRY. I WILL COME AND VISIT YOU LATER.

Luc

– Yes, come when you can, as often as possible.

Monique

– NO! YOU MUST MAKE A NEW LIFE FOR YOURSELF. I WILL COME ONLY TO GIVE YOU STRENGTH; THIS IS THE WAY MY LOVE MUST BE.

Luc

– This I accept.

Monique

– NOW I WANT TO WALK AROUND THIS PLACE AND GO NEAR MY HUSBAND. THEN YOU CAN HELP ME LEAVE. MY BABY IS WAITING, AND THEY WILL HELP ME. THANK YOU, AND ESPECIALLY THIS PERSON.

Carole

– Jocelyne?

Monique

– YES. NOW I WILL WALK AROUND!

Carole

– Walk around, and then let us know when you are ready.

Monique

– LUC, YOU MUST FORGET MY PRESENCE IN OUR BED! DO YOU UNDERSTAND?

Luc

– Yes, I promise that after you have gone I will try to change the whole house. It will be hard, but I will try.

Monique

– YES, THAT'S A GOOD DECISION, I APPROVE. I WILL WATCH FROM ABOVE AND I WILL GUIDE YOU. AND MAY MY THOUGHTS BE POSITIVE FOR YOU.

Carole

– Luc has very good memories of your life together. He still loves you very much.

Monique

– I AM NEAR HIM!

Luc

– Put your hand on my shoulder so I can feel your presence. You promise to come and see me when you can, to help me?

Monique

– NOT BEFORE A FEW MONTHS. I AM READY NOW, THANK YOU!

Carole

– You are going to walk into this Light which is moving up! You will see people who are coming to help you. You will see hands held out to help you go up, my love! Go into the Light.

Monique

– IT IS SO DIFFICULT!

Carole

– Yes, it is hard! Move into this Light and go towards God; God is at the top of the Light! You will feel fine up there; you will find happiness, another kind of happiness.

Monique

– THIS MEANS I MUST LET GO OF WHAT WAS!

Carole

– That's right! Come back now and then to give strength to Luc, but continue on your pathway. You will come back another time.

Monique

– I AM STARTING TO MOVE FAR AWAY FROM YOU.

Luc

– Monique, don't worry about your body. I will take care of it.

Monique

– MY FACE! THERE'S NO FACE LEFT.

Carole

– It's only a physical body, and Luc will close the casket; so it's not important, Monique.

Monique

– I KNOW.

Luc

– I will have you buried with grandpa and grandma. Does this please you?

Monique

– IT'S NOT IMPORTANT.

Carole

– Are you continuing in the Light?

Monique

– YES, I AM BEGINNING TO ABANDON MY BODY; I DON'T HAVE ANY MORE PAIN.

Carole

– Continue to go upwards! Your baby is waiting for you up there. Keep going up towards your baby. Keep going up with the Light.

We were all very relieved that she had finally accepted to go on her soul path! I knew that for awhile she would be in a place of rest, taken care of by loving souls whose task it was to help the ones in distress, once they had accepted their situation. Luc kept busy with his work, occupying his leisure time the best he could, considering the circumstances, always impatiently waiting for news that they had found Monique's body.

On the 21st of April, during a seance in my advanced class, Monique made an appearance again through Jocelyne, who was in a state of trance. She came in, bringing with her a soul who had also committed suicide a few months before, and whose body had still not been recovered. This person was related to someone who was also a part of the course, and was present that night. She said she had "dragged" Rachel in for us to help, as she had been helped.

Monique then shared with us her experiences before and after her passing:

"I thank you Madame, and the instrument (Jocelyne), for the help that you gave me, because this allowed me to have a last look at the place where I lived with my husband and my child. I also thank you because this permitted my husband to let go of me. As you know, I no longer have an earthly envelope and only my soul exists. My physical body suffered also; your instrument felt the suffering I went through to pay for my action.

"I would like to tell all of you that God does not easily accept it when we make the decision to terminate our life on this Earth! I took my child with me. I want to thank you Madame, for having hidden this fact from me, for at the moment I asked you about him, my soul was not ready to accept this sad reality. Because of the help you gave me, I have now left my physical body behind, and have entered the dimension which separates me from the earth plane. I am aware now, because it was my child who met me!

"As you know, we have to answer to God, and everyone is subject to this fact – that is His justice! It is our subconscious which holds all of our actions from the day of our birth, until the moment we leave this world, and God asks us the reason for breaking his Spiritual Laws, His Commandments. He asks us for humility, and to live our lives better; to look for happiness where we are, rather than running away, which is what I did. I resigned from life in a gesture of discouragement. Also having lived so intensely close to my husband and being selfishly in love, I thought that this child took his love away from me. I was very negative, the type of person who believed and expected the worst before it happened. Also, I had a great need for the other person to be close to me. Maybe the fact that my husband had a strong personality and I a weak one, overwhelmed me sometimes. I am not here to expose my life to you or to judge, but so you can understand the situation.

"I've often asked myself why I did such a thing. Maybe a need for attention. Revenge against those close to me... A way to make them regret my absence... It's like I had to take a decisive step so they would hurt, feel sorrow, so they would notice that I existed. I succeeded! But what harm I did to myself also! When I wanted to change my mind, stop the gesture, it was too late!

"Before, we are in a sort of euphoria, where everything leads up to this; we think only of this! We think everyone else is wrong and we are the only one who is right. We think that leaving this world will bring us other joys, and also that a miracle will happen at the last minute which will change everything. Unfortunately, it is not so! My loved ones are there crying, they are hurting, and so am I!

"I also want to tell you that no matter what trials and tribulations we have in our lives, no matter what happens, we are never alone. Sometimes we say, We don't have anyone to talk to about it. It's partly true, but it's partly false. If we talk to people close to us, they are concerned with their own problems and don't give us satisfaction. They don't say the phrases we absolutely want to hear; sometimes to be told that we are wrong, and sometimes to be told that we are right. But sometimes to tell us exactly how it is. *Change yourself* !; It's fine to say *Change yourself*, but there are moments when we feel alone and lonely, and have lost interest in everything. We suddenly feel in a world completely apart from everyone else.

"To be told: *Others succeeded! Others did this! Others did that; so why can't you?* only makes us feel pushed down. We think that it must be true, if others succeeded, why can't we? The questions just go around and around! That really doesn't help, because it just makes you feel more inadequate. You feel as if you're being watched, you feel judged. I have to say that it's not only that which made me commit the act I did; let's say it all started long before. But that's not what I want to talk about.

"From the dimension where I was, I saw myself drowned, and I followed my husband home to help him. It was painful, but it depends on the acceptance; because only God is permitted to sever our ties with the Earth, and only He can decide when the time is right to do so.

"When you came to my home I was jealous. That was one of my faults. I worried about your presence there, as I didn't easily accept people whom I didn't know. But then I understood that if Luc held you in high esteem, and allowed you in my home, it was to help reassure him, and to help me accept what had happened. I thank you, because I found peace. I already feel much better; and if I am able, by my words, to encourage one woman (I say woman because I was a woman) to continue to hope, in spite of her doubts, that she will find the help and support she desperately needs. Communication is so important in a family, but unfortunately it doesn't always work! We want to talk, the other one doesn't listen. We talk, but sometimes they don't give us the answers we need to hear; and then we become impatient, then aggressive, and we feel sorry for ourselves. We say: "Why wait? What will waiting change?" Sometimes we commit an act like this because we always need the other person around us. Sometimes, but not always, we have been selfishly spoiled! We manipulate a man, and if he slips away from us, we can no longer face the reality of life. Sometimes we live our entire lives around a man, and the rest is not important. We suffocate him, and then we find ourselves in a different situation. We wake up, but it is too late; the other one has a desire to run away from this prison. Sometimes it's this way for certain people who attempt this desperate act. Other times it's to draw attention to get the help we need.

"Most of all, I thank you for helping me to understand that this world I lived in, everything I loved – my personal things, my clothes, the things I loved the most – no longer have any importance. We have to leave everything behind! The things I bought when we travelled, all my gifts, what value I put on all those material things! But now it's another life.

"You are probably curious to know a little about this other life! So was I! I was so curious that I made a hasty decision to find out! (She says this with a little laugh and I could see acceptance and the progress she had made since her passing.) As you know, I drowned myself! During the seconds I was facing this reality, it was a shock. I fought and tried to come back up to the surface. Then the water was above my head and I started to choke. After, I was in a state of shock and saw myself slowly leave my body. We walk on the ground... we want to enter our house; we want to continue living like before, but we are surrounded by a wall of indifference. Everyone is crying. There is so much sorrow and we wonder why, seeing that we are there. We are right beside them, but can't reach them. We wander like lost souls, wondering what is happening; why, all of a sudden, we can't even talk to anyone.

"As you know, we can stay in this state of being for a long time. Then, at some point, things seem to clear a little around us; and someone asks us if we want to leave this world. Unfortunately it's not easy to say that we want to leave this world that has fascinated us for so long, because we are attached to the physical, material things. But it's not exactly at the moment of death that all this happens. Our body stays behind for a certain time, but our soul continues; and someone like me, who took her own life, must face this reality!

"Certain people don't have the same torments. I am at the stage where I must accept the reality, and this has nothing to do with whether my body has been recovered or not. It's as if God is making me go through different stages, which are forcing me to reflect on this gift of life he had given me, and that I had decided to cut short. Those of you who are women, whether you have children or not, no matter what happens, if you can't find help from someone close to you, please look outside the home for a person willing to let you talk about your fears and insecurities. Some of you who are stubborn and don't want to change, but get exasperated from everyone telling you *do this! do that!*, should take a second look at your wrong attitudes. Accept to make the changes necessary for the well-being of the whole family. Some people want everything to happen instantly; but if it's not the right time, it won't happen. You need to learn patience. You need to have at least one close friend in your life, with whom you can get together once a week, and share your problems for mutual support. This is my greatest wish for each of you. No matter who the person is at your side in your personal life, if you can only say one good word of encouragement, do so. If you are the one who needs the encouraging words, that you may also receive them.

"As I have told you before, I have acquired a sense of peace. I was tormented; but, having been able to talk to you gives me even greater peace. I hope to have been able to help some of you with my words. I want to encourage you, and make you realize that you are privileged, because you are still on Earth. In spite of your worries and disappointments in life, the more hope you have, the sooner things can change if you make the effort."

I asked if she had a message for Luc.

"Not for the moment, because I am helping him the best I can. I especially want him to forget me, but it is not easy. I want him to go forward with a positive attitude, so that he looks at life in a new way, releasing the bitterness and letting his heart open once again to love. I know it's a lot to ask of him, following the tragedy in his life, but I want him to leave the door open to joy; that he find peace of mind, because there is no reason for him to feel self-reproach. I am with him often to help.

"What I have shared with you is to make you understand that sometimes we are really mixed up, and we refuse the help; or if we have it, it doesn't satisfy us. I hope I have been able to express properly what I wanted to say. Also

I wanted to ask you if you would accept that I come back to talk to you now and then, to help me advance faster. (Anytime you like, Monique.) But Luc must not try to reach me for the time being, because I am at a stage where I must accept leaving everything behind; sort of like a nun who must leave the past behind to dedicate her life to God.

"I know they are still searching for my physical body, but it won't change anything for me when it is found. Luc is looking for answers; he thinks the doctor may not have been attentive to me and my needs. (Luc had taken the first tape to Monique's doctor, and had him listen to it in its entirety. He seemed stunned, and admitted that it did sound very much like the way she talked, but of course he would not say anything else.) But even if this tragedy only serves to help him, and other doctors like him, to become more aware when another man or woman who is planning to do the same thing I did come to them for help; that they may hear their silent cry, because we don't always express it properly, and a lot of today's doctors don't take the time to listen.

"Luc is torturing himself. He thinks, "Maybe I didn't do this, maybe I should have done that". He constantly tries to analyze the situation, but the fact that escapes him is: *That it was my decision!* So tell him to close the door on the act that I committed. The how, the why, it will change absolutely nothing!

"I have told you a little of my story, but I will keep the heart of the problem to myself as atonement for what I did, also for my detachment from the Earth. And for Luc, because I want him to be at peace. Please keep me in the Light to help me advance faster. *I wish you all peace!*"

The soul that Monique had brought to us for rescuing was a very hard case, because she was still in her physical body in the water and didn't want to leave it. Rachel had been a very down to earth person, whose physical body and material possessions were the most important things in her life, sometimes to the detriment of her children. Her looks were of the utmost importance, and her whole life revolved around that fact.

Rachel was very upset that she was in the water surrounded by garbage, in an area of the river which was very dirty. We worked very hard to convince her that she had to leave her body, because she was no longer on the physical plane. She knew what she had done, and told us she had waited for a moment when the family stopped watching her, and then had made her move. Rachel had always been very stubborn, and when she made up her mind to do something, always went through with it. We explained that we were there to help her, but she had to help herself as well. She argued for a period of time and was finally convinced that she had no other alternative. The fact that she was so disgusted with the dirty environment in which she found herself helped her make the decision.

Rachel's strong attachment to her physical body made it very difficult for her to see the white Light, which both we and the Spirit World were projecting to her. We finally asked her mother and father on the other side to come and help her, as we thought it might be easier for her to connect with them, rather than with the Light. Someone who has no knowledge of the Spirit World except what they have learned in Orthodox Churches, and have not evolved to a greater degree soulwise, often have more difficulty making the transition, especially in situations like this one.

Rachel was worried about how she would look when they found the body, as she could see herself and was aware that she no longer had a face. We explained over and over that the physical body was no longer of any importance, and that it was imperative that she move out of her body and try to see the Light. The Spirit World realized that they had a problem, because at some point Rachel asked if she should grasp the rope which was being lowered to her. We were very happy to say: "Yes, and start climbing, and don't stop until you reach the top!"

We had told Rachel at the beginning that Monique had brought her to us for help, and she wanted to know who she was. We said that she was someone who had done the same thing she had, and we had helped her also. Monique came in a couple of times to tell us not to ask any questions, that Rachel was very traumatized and confused; but to get her over as soon as possible. She stayed hanging on the rope for about fifteen minutes, and was having a bad time. She kept asking her mother and father to help her. But the fact that she was so earthbound in her thoughts kept her from moving up at a faster pace, because "passing over" can be done in an instant when we accept to do so mentally. Rachel wanted to be reassured that her husband would continue searching for her body until it was found, and was worried about the fact that it wouldn't be pretty, because she said that she had always tried to keep herself looking pretty for him. We told her that he would understand, and would take care of everything; and to stop worrying about that part of her life.

Finally Monique came in to tell us that it was over, and that she had been taken away to a place of rest. We were all very relieved. She said good night and thanked us once again! She said she would see us soon, of which I had no doubt!

On the 2nd of June Monique paid us a last visit. As on the preceding one, she excused herself for the fact that she had "pushed herself in" before Jocelyne was in a deeper state of trance, but she wanted to make sure she would be able to come through. I recognized her immediately from the intonation of her voice, as each one is different, and someone you know is easy to recognize.

She was in a very happy state, and started by saying:

"I want to tell you that I have been given special permission to bring my little baby with me! (Throughout most of the conversation, she held her arms in the way she would if she were holding a baby.) My heart was torn, because what happened was not what I really wanted for him!

"I want to say thank you from the bottom of my heart for the help you gave me. I am much more relaxed; I have a calmness I would have liked to have had while living on Earth. I have been given an incredible blessing! Maybe because I helped others, God has permitted me to go directly to another dimension, where I can once again take up my role as a mother to my child! It's like a huge nursery where we learn not to play mother, but to participate in acquiring the understanding that we lacked while on Earth.

"I sometimes see my ex-husband, because I would like him to be happy and have a new life, possibly start another family. (I marveled at the evolution of this little soul in such a short period of time! To have gone from the insecure person she was on Earth, to the total acceptance of her new life, and having detached herself to this degree from everything she held dear!) This attitude must be part of my new life. Before, I would have had great difficulty accepting that fact, especially when I can see him. But where I am now, I am like a caretaker of children; where I prepare them to come back to earth in a new body. I can't tell you much because, for the moment, I don't know everything about the tasks they have given me in my new life. All I can say is that it is very beautiful where I am, and I am very happy to have my son with me once again.

"You remember Rachel, the woman I brought to you for help? (Yes.) Well, she's going to have to do a lot of climbing! (Has she advanced a little?) Yes, a little, and I am helping her from here. She really drowned, although I think her family still doubts that fact. They should find her in a short period of time, before the summer is over. It will be by chance, because her body is in an area where it is almost impossible to surface. They will have difficulty recognizing her, but it will happen. She will not be coming to visit you because she is at a stage of total revolt, and we prefer to help her on this side, rather than bothering you.

"This is all I have come to say tonight, but I wanted to share my new found happiness with you and show you my son. Tell Jocelyne I am sorry about my abruptness at pushing my way in before she was ready to start, but there are so many people lined up waiting that I was afraid a little person like me wouldn't have a chance! All those big guys! (I knew she was talking about the Guides.) If you could only see the Light around this house, all the people coming in and out, and the number of them standing around and watching! I had to almost sneak through the big guys' legs on my hands and knees to get in first!" (She said laughingly.)

Monique's body was finally located sometime during the month of May of that same year. Because it was a year which brought with it a very cold winter and a late Spring, the ice in the river was especially thick and took a long time to melt. Luc kept his promise and went to identify the body himself. He told me that it wasn't the shock he had expected, for he knew that the Monique he had known and loved was no longer in that body. Following Luc's first visit to me, he had taken my courses. He now saw life from a completely different perspective than before, and had evolved spiritually in his own way. I am happy to say that he did start a new life for himself, as Monique had wanted; but I don't think he planned on having another child.

When someone goes through a traumatic situation such as this in their life, there is no way they can ever be the same! Either we come out of it stronger with a greater faith in God, because at some point in the experience we have nothing to hang onto but the thought that there must be a reason for this; or we can go the other way, blaming everybody but ourselves, and holding onto the bitterness for the rest of our lives. We have the choice to advance or to regress in our soul growth through every experience given to us. ***This is our God given right: Free Will!***

Chapter Five

HAUNTED HOUSE IN THE LAURENTIANS

In July 1984, two young men bought a house together in the Laurentians, a well known ski resort area north of Montreal, Quebec, Canada. They each had a business in the small town, and were away from the house all day long. Their home was a beautifully decorated two story Swiss Chalet type, both men having a lot of creativity.

Jean was alone at home the first week. He felt very lonely, as the place was situated about two miles from the town. Sitting on the sofa, feeling a little sorry for himself, he suddenly felt the presence of someone sitting beside him. The energy around him changed completely, and he no longer felt alone. From that point on, his sense of loneliness disappeared.

At the beginning of July, the key chains which held the house and car keys started to disappear. They would hang them on a nail in the cupboard on arriving home, only to be found at the bottom of the clothes hamper. This happened about four times over a period of two months. At the beginning of August, a pair of work boots, which had been put away in the closet, disappeared. This was followed a few days later by a belt which was hanging in its usual place.

In September, Jean's mother came for a visit and decided to stay overnight in the guest room downstairs. The men installed a night light for her in the hall, as their room was on the second level. The next morning she told them that the light kept flashing on and off during the night.

Gilles awakened Jean one night and asked him if he could hear the noises in the house, but Jean heard nothing. Both men were very sensitive, but Gilles had great mediumship potential and was even more open. They started to hear the strange noises more frequently, which always seemed to be coming from downstairs. The living room and dining room were one huge room, with the ceiling open to the roof; and there was a beautiful big chandelier hanging over the dining room table.

One night, around the end of February, Jean was watching television when it suddenly changed channels. On a Saturday night in April, he went to his closet to get a coat, and it was no longer there. He remembered having seen it hanging in its usual place a week before. A few days later they were both awakened at 4:00 a.m. by noises that sounded as if someone were knocking on the wall of their bedroom. It was two sharp knocks, followed by ten to fifteen seconds of silence, and then repeated. It happened three times in a row. Then they could hear several people whispering.

At the beginning of May, Jean was awakened by noises and the dog immediately started to bark. He heard very soft laughter, as if some women were enjoying themselves immensely; but he said that it didn't sound natural. Telepathically he told them he was tired and to let him sleep. The next morning his friend Gilles told him that he had never slept so soundly! But they had a surprise waiting for them.

The T.V. was turned on to a channel that didn't exist on the cable, and the screen was blank except for the snow. Also, the ceiling fan had been turned off!

Other strange things happened, such as setting the switch for the outdoor lights to come on at dusk when they left for the evening, and coming home to a house in darkness. The lights would all come on the minute they walked in the door! During the same period, for three consecutive days they would get up in the morning to find the T.V. on and the channel changer on channel 88. This channel did not exist on the T.V.

A week later, Gilles told Jean that he had asked the spirits to prove they existed, but not to scare him. The next morning he went to get a sweater which had been washed, folded and put on the shelf in the closet. As he took it out he saw that a large hole, about three by five inches, had been burned in the middle of the front. It was at this point I was called in to help.

They were really freaking out over this incident, as I think any normal person would. Jean's mother had seen the T.V. programs I had done with Pierre Milot, and called him to get my phone number. Jean explained part of what was happening over the phone, and we made an appointment for them to come to my house that same week. I was giving a class that night, so I invited them to participate if they wished. I also asked him to bring the sweater and a resume of all that had happened up until then.

Jean arrived with his mother and his sister, and we sat down to discuss the situation. He showed me the sweater; and of course, as I usually do, I tried to eliminate all other possibilities for the burn. I asked him if he had ironed the sweater, and he said yes, but he never used a hot iron. I knew it had been burned by a fire of some kind because of the blackened area around the hole, so I asked him if he smoked when he did the ironing. He said yes, but he was sure he had not dropped his cigarette or ashes on the sweater. As I examined it closely, I knew that this phenomenon had to be spirit controlled. It had been neatly folded; and the lining of the back, which was white, had not a speck of black from the large burn on the front, even though the two pieces had to be touching while it was burning. *Gilles had asked for proof, and Spirit had obliged him!*

On the 30th of May, I went up to St. Sauveur with Irene Griffey, who was staying with me for a few days while doing seances for my students. I wanted to try to go into trance and do the rescue myself, while Irene would serve as control.

We arrived at 2:00 p.m. and talked for a few minutes with Jean and his mother, who had joined us for the day. I started to discern in every room of the house. As I went into the only bedroom on the second floor, psychically I saw a thin man with gray hair smoking a pipe, which could have been symbolic for a very calm and poised person. He was standing in the corner of the room, and immediately I knew that he had died of a heart attack.

We installed two chairs facing each other. Then we lit a candle in front of me to serve as the Light to which we would try to convince the spirit to go. I proceeded to go into my trance state, which took about ten minutes. Strong Bow came through first for protection and to give the blessing. He then announced that they would bring the spirit through.

I heard a cracking sound in the corner; and, with my inner eye, I saw him approaching my body from the back, and felt him enter in the area at the bottom of my skull. He asked what we were doing in his house. He said that his wife had died in that house. Somehow I "knew" he was seventy-two years old and that his wife had died at the age of fifty-six. I also psychically saw that there had been two children, a boy and a girl.

Irene started talking to him, explaining that he had passed from his physical body, and he was to go to the Light situated in front of him. He peered in front of him as if he were seeing something, and then said, "my wife and children are here", and started to cry. He sobbed for about five minutes, until my mascara was running down my face. Finally composing himself, he said he was going with them. I felt, and psychically saw him leave my body through my solar plexus, and go towards them. They all turned their backs and started to slowly ascend into the Light. Suddenly he turned and waved, and they all disappeared from sight. I called two days later and talked to Gilles. He said that all was quiet, and that the whole atmosphere of the house had changed.

I had just started to write down my experience at their home when the phone rang! It was Jean, and he said that they had just returned from a trip to Quebec City. On arriving home, the television was turned on to a non-existent channel and the chandelier over the dining room table was all lit up. They knew they had turned everything off in the house before leaving on their trip. I told them I would go back as soon as I could!

I went back three weeks later, and planned to stay overnight to finish the job started a month before. Jean's mother and father, both very intuitive and interested in the spiritual and psychic field, were there. Frank Beauchamp and Pauline Rainville, both excellent mediums from Montreal, arrived in the evening to assist me. Frank had worked with me on other cases, and they did some work together on their own. We all sat and talked for a few minutes. Frank suddenly asked Pauline to tune in and see who was standing beside him, as he felt a presence very strongly! She described a woman wearing old fashioned clothes and a shawl over her shoulders. Pauline mentally asked her why she was there. She replied that she was attracted to the house because of the wood, (the whole house was built of pine wood, from the floors to the ceilings), but that she didn't make any noise or bother anyone. Jean wanted her to leave, as Gilles was very frightened of it all, and was becoming depressed. She said that she had no intention of leaving, and scurried to the end of the hall. The huge chandelier had been gently swinging for at least fifteen minutes, and I asked someone to turn off the fan to see if this was the cause; but ten minutes later it was still moving. Pauline tuned in, and said a young man was swinging on the long chain going to the ceiling. She gave us his description and asked him to leave. The swinging slowly stopped.

Later in the evening, we decided to do a seance and I would go into trance. After discerning upstairs, I went downstairs to get my briefcase which contained the things I always brought with me when I worked. As I walked back upstairs, there was a very strong odor of a candle burning on the open landing. No one had lit a candle at that point, as mine were still in my bag. It seemed that someone in the Spirit World was prepared before we were!

We were in the bedroom with the family members sitting on the bed watching. Frank was controlling, which meant he was the one who would talk to them as they came in.

Three or four spirits came through, including a ninety-four year old man named David. He was dying in a hospital somewhere, but was afraid to let go. Probably in a coma, his spirit was traveling out of the body. He begged them for help, and Frank told him to go to the Light, it was time to leave his physical body, because it was no longer of any use to him. Gilles and Jean both said later that when he left my body, they saw a flash of beautiful blue light. Just as I was coming out of trance, there were two sharp raps on the wall beside Frank and me. This was my first experience with hearing raps, about which I had read so much! He asked them to give another signal, but they didn't.

I knew that there were many other spirits in the house and that there was still a lot of work to be done, but I didn't tell the men. They had sold the house during the three weeks between visits, and I hoped there wouldn't be too many problems before they were to leave a month later!

When everyone had left, Gilles shared with me what had happened two days before. Knowing that I planned to sleep over that night to do a little research, they had made up the bed in the guest room downstairs in preparation for my visit. That morning Gilles had gone in to see that everything was ready, and received the surprise of his life! The bed was stripped, with the bedclothes pulled down and laying on the floor at the foot of the bed. There was an indentation in the pillow, as if someone had slept there.

It was after 1:00 a.m. before I got to bed. I put my tape recorder on in the living room, planning to leave it there for a couple of hours to see if I could pick up some spirit voices or other phenomena. I had been overworking as I often did, and was very tired. I had only been asleep a short while when I felt my bed being shaken by someone standing at the foot. Mentally I told them not to bother me as I was tired. A few minutes later there were two sharp raps on my door, and it opened by itself. I could hear the excited laughter of what sounded like several little children, and I mentally told them to go play somewhere else. They were only a group of little spirits having some fun. Another trance medium, working over a period of time, would be needed to convince them all to leave the house. Because the house had been sold, I decided to leave the problem up to the new owners!

I was convinced that the men, especially Jean, had unknowingly permitted them to manifest, for they were both open channels. I had taken a small book of daily readings called "God Calling" with me, which was like my Bible. When I came home, it had disappeared out of my suitcase. They had the last laugh on me after all!

Gilles and Jean, had made an offer to buy the house, and submitted what they thought was a low bid, expecting the owner to negotiate a higher price. However, they were surprised to have their offer accepted immediately, since it was twenty thousand dollars less than what the owner had paid the year before! He told them that he was selling because the stairs were too much for his wife. A week later the wife came by to bring an extra key, and she said they had sold because she was too nervous in the house!

The afternoon that I was there, Jean and I went to examine the records at the town hall and were told that the place had changed hands four or five times in the eight years it had been built. We then went to see the farmer who had owned the land on which the house was built, as he knew everyone who had lived there. We especially wanted to know if anyone had died in the house, but he said no.

During the summer months this area is a favorite place where my husband loved to go and spend a day in the mountains. One day I went with him, and pointed out "my haunted house". Being the skeptic that he is, he started to argue that "if it were true, everyone would know about it, and it would be in the newspapers!" Of course I told him that when you have a house that is really haunted; "You keep your mouth shut, and get it on the market and sold as fast as possible. Otherwise, you won't even be able to give it away!" I knew that, at some point, a "spiritual passageway" had been opened in that house; and I felt that this was possibly done by someone who had lived there who had played with a ouija board, or done automatic writing, and had not known how to protect themselves. The group of spirits who came in and out of the place were not malevolent; and a person less sensitive than my two friends probably would hardly have noticed them except for feeling strange at times, and the cracking noises. For uninvited spirits to be able to manifest, they need the right energy, and are nurtured by the emotions. Someone who is fearful gives them the energy to be even stronger, and this is so for both kinds, good and bad. Someone, possibly unknow-ingly, opened a door at some time. Otherwise they would not have been there!

My husband fell in love with the house, and since 1985 has been going up to admire it from the outside at least once a year. Each Spring there has been a new "For Sale" sign on the lawn. We know it has changed hands three times since my visits, and last year the sign went up again. He talked to the agent, and asked him why the owners were selling. He replied: "They only told me that there were noises in the house!"

Chapter Six

THE LADY IN THE LAKE

In chapter three, I mentioned that I would have reason to remember the words of the guide concerning the murderer of the children who had been sent to us for soul rescue.

On the 10th of October, 1982, our Canadian Thanksgiving weekend, I was at Bernard's house where we were holding a seance. It was the usual family group, including his sister-in-law Diane, who was sitting with us for the first time.

We prepared, as usual, with meditation and prayer. Suddenly Diane began to panic, saying she felt something close to her that wanted to overpower her. She was very frightened. We knew it was a soul that needed help, and we tried to convince her to let the Spirit express itself through her; but she was too afraid. So we sent her to sit in another room until she could compose herself.

Bernard then went into trance. A soul came through who said he was a guide for someone he had brought to us for help, but that she spoke only English. The Spirit then tried to channel through Bernard in English, and was able to find a few words to express herself; but she was very frustrated, as it was difficult for her. (I think it's important to explain that if mediums are in a **very deep** trance state, where they are completely out of their bodies, a spirit can speak any language. But if we are in a light or medium trance, where we are still in the body, or standing beside it and have knowledge of what is being said through us, the soul has to use the language we have in our subconscious minds.) The guides who are experienced in channeling can usually find the words needed to make themselves understood, but it is very difficult for a soul coming through for the first time, especially in such a confused and emotional state as she was.

Spirit
— IT'S VERY IMPORTANT THAT I GIVE MY MESSAGE!

Carole
— Who is the message for?

Spirit
— MY LITTLE BOY.

Carole
— What is his name?

Spirit
— PATRICK.

Carole
— Where does he live?

Spirit
— I DON'T KNOW.

Carole
— It's important that you give us the information so we can reach him to deliver the message. What is your name?

Spirit
— ELIZABETH MORROW (or Moreau).

Carole
— Is Patrick's name also Morrow?

Spirit
— No.

Carole
— Do you remember his last name?

Spirit

  — IT'S HARD TO SPEAK.

Carole

  — You're doing just fine. Can you give us the message?

Spirit

  — I WAS KIDNAPPED WITH MY BOY!

Carole

  — Is Patrick your boy?

Spirit

  — YES. (very distressed)... HE PUT ME IN A BAG AND PUT ME IN THE WATER!

Carole

  — Where did you live?

Spirit

  — MY BOY! (She was having a hard time explaining because of the language barrier, and was very upset.)

At this point her guide came in and said that they could not use Bernard. He didn't have enough English in his subconscious mind for her to be able to find the words necessary to tell us what had happened to her.

Carole

  — Ginette has a little more knowledge of English. Could she use her instead?

Guide

  — She must accept, as I cannot serve as an intermediary for her because she is too confused. It is easier for her to express herself, but this medium does not have enough notions of the English language.

Carole

  — You can't translate for her?

Guide
- It is impossible because of the state of confusion she is in. I am one of her guides, but she was not prepared for this horrible death! I will try to push her to use the other instrument.

While we were waiting for her guide to convince her to control Ginette, Bernard could psychically see the body in a large bag in the water. I asked him if he could get any of the details, and he decided to astrally project himself to where it was. He came out of the water to look around. I asked him to look for a sign or something that would give us some indication of where he was. He sounded strange and said he was drawn towards the bag, but I firmly directed him *to move away from it,* and to look around for other clues as to the whereabouts of the body. The soul came back through Bernard and said three men had done it. I asked if she knew their names and she said, "Buck. He's dangerous! He's crazy! There's no longer any danger for me."

Carole
- It's O.K., it's finished; but I want you to tell me where you can be found.

Spirit
- CLOSE TO THE SHORE OF A BIG RIVER, NEAR A SUMMER CAMP.

Bernard came in to give us the details of what he was seeing: "I'm in a wooded area."

Carole
- Is it in the Province of Quebec? (We are within 5 miles of the Ontario border.) Look for a sign on the side of the road, the nearest one you can find, and try to read it.

Bernard
- There are three guys and a beautiful little boy with blonde hair about three years old in that shack! Oh! They

have just sensed my presence! There is a police car not too far away.

Carole

— What is it doing there?

Bernard

— I'll go and sit with them.

Carole

— Ask them where they are from and what station they work out of.

Bernard

— It has blue flashers on the top. It's like a police car, but the flashers are blue.

Carole

— Could they be game wardens? Ask them where they are from.

Bernard

— They don't answer me. (Being in his astral body, this was being asked telepathically; but they were not open to this type of communication.)

Carole

— Get out of the car and continue on the road, because we absolutely need a name of some kind.

Bernard

— It's an Ontario license plate on the car.

Carole

— Keep looking for a road sign and move ahead faster.

Bernard

— There is a sign which says "Throwing garbage is prohibited".

At this moment the Spirit controlled Ginette, and came in crying and very upset. She was trying to find the words in English.

Spirit

– IT'S THE SAME...YOU KNOW THE ONE...THE MAN THAT YOU HAVE A "GANT" (glove)!

Carole

– The one who killed the young girls?

Spirit

– YES! YES! IT'S THE SAME ONE! GO TO MY LITTLE BOY PATRICK! (She's very emotional and sobs.)

Carole

– Where is he? You have to tell us where he is!

Spirit

– IN ONTARIO.

Carole

– You have to tell us the address, sweetheart! At what address is he?

Spirit

– (Crying) I DON'T KNOW...MY BOY...MY LITTLE BOY...

Carole

– But we have to know where you are.

Spirit

– YOU KNOW WHERE THERE IS A CAMPING...(She was trying hard to find the English words to describe the area, and we were unable to understand; so she pointed to Robert and said, "He goes there often," and Robert asked if it was Upper Canada Village. She sobbed, "Yes! Yes! Yes! Please go!", relieved at having been able to give us some indication of the region where it happened, and possibly where her son could be found.)

Carole

– Can you give us more details? (Still very nervous and trembling, she tried her best to tell us what she could.)

Spirit

— THEY HAVE A RED VAN WITH A LOT OF PUTTY ON IT IN MANY PLACES. (We finally understood that they had been doing some body work on the van, and the red she was describing was the primer coat of paint.)

Carole

— That's the color of the car the men have, but where is your little boy?

Spirit

— I DON'T KNOW. HE IS WITH HIM, AND HE PUT ME IN THE BAG IN THE WATER BECAUSE I FOUGHT HIM. HE PUT THE BAG IN CEMENT, AND PUSHED ME IN THE WATER!

Carole

— We want to know where your body is.

Spirit

— I DON'T KNOW, BECAUSE HE BLINDFOLDED ME AND I AM SO CONFUSED; BUT I LIVED NEAR UPPER CANADA VILLAGE.

Carole

— Is it a river or a lake?

Spirit

— I DON'T KNOW... I AM SO COLD! IT'S NOT IMPORTANT FOR ME. MY BOY IS IMPORTANT... GO TO FIND HIM, O.K.?

Carole

— We are going to help your little boy, but we want to help you also.

Spirit

— No! No! I'M NOT IMPORTANT; THE GUIDES WILL TAKE CARE OF ME. GO AND FIND MY LITTLE BOY! I'M NOT IMPORTANT; MY LITTLE BOY IS IMPORTANT! HURRY UP!

Carole
- You said your last name was Moreau; Can you tell me your first name again?

Spirit
- IT'S NOT IMPORTANT; WHAT IS IMPORTANT IS MY LITTLE BOY! HELP HIM!

During all of this time, Bernard had stayed in his trance state. He was still projecting himself to the area astrally, to see what he could find. He saw some dogs and a few other things. At this moment, a guide came through Ginette, speaking English.

Guide
- This message is very important. I will try to describe what I see. There is a cottage near the water and there are three men in it. A van with a coat of primer paint is parked in the yard. There is a lot of firewood, and some of it is piled up; and the axe is still stuck in one piece of wood. The police are coming close to the place, and are preparing to arrest them.

While the whole scenario was going on, Bernard and I could psychically follow their every move, and the rescue of Patrick. What intrigued me was the fact that the police cars had blue lights on top! When it was over, we decided to take a break and moved to the kitchen. I needed some answers, and called the nearest Provincial Police Station across the border in Ontario. I asked the officer if anything was happening at the moment, and he asked "such as what?". I told him I was a medium, and we were having a seance. We were getting some information about a murder and a kidnapping. He said no, all was quiet, and there was nothing like that happening. I told him that I was not a "kook", but a well-known business woman in the area where I lived, and gave him my name and address. I had a last question for him. "What color are the lights on the roof of your police cars?" He answered red. I then asked him what would be blue, and he said that the only thing that had blue lights were the snowplows. When I hung up, I felt angry. I wondered what was happening, as Ginette, Bernard and I followed their every move psychically; and we all saw the same thing. I said immediately, "Let's go back into the seance room, because I need some answers!" The guides, knowing me so well and having been conscious of our conversations during the break, came through the moment Ginette sat down!

Guide

– This is a phenomenon that happened a few days ago. It was an unmarried mother, and she had bought too many drugs without paying for them, and they "settled the account"! But now she has awakened, and she has come here. They have not found the child yet; all the details are right, but he has not been found. We sent all of you on an astral trip for the scenario, because the mother was here continually, and heard everything that was said. Now that she has seen this, she at least **believes** that her son has been found, and has now gone for a rest on our side. The little boy has not really been rescued, but all the details you have are right, the red van with the patches, and the small cottage. The only thing we added were the police, so that the mother would believe that he was found. You've already had enough problems without having her on your back all the time; because she would not have left you alone until she was sure he was safe. I believe that the police force will get in contact with you. We are very thankful for your collaboration.

Carole

– Were they really the same ones who murdered the little girls?

Guide

— Yes.

Carole

— Do they still live in the Montreal area?

Guide

— Yes, they do, but they were on a little trip.

Carole

— Where did the young woman live?

Guide

— In that area, around Cornwall.

Carole

— Is the little boy alright?

Guide

— For the time being, but he is not treated too well. He doesn't eat properly, but it's not too bad.

Carole

— Do you have any other names to give us besides Veilleux?

Guide

— Gauthier! But we will try to get more information and let you know.

Carole

— And I will be getting a call from the police?

Guide

— Oh yes! That is what we told you! We are very happy to see the wonderful work you are all doing together, hand in hand. Try to listen to us when we talk to you, at least a little (laughter), because we are close. But there is still the lady who cried when she tried to come through the other instrument at the beginning of the seance.

Carole

— She is not the same one?

Guide

— No! She is a woman who stayed caught for awhile between Heaven and Earth because she didn't want to understand; but now she does, and wanted to say she was sorry. She hasn't gone over yet because she has to talk; she was the one who cried while controlling Diane.

Carole

— Does she still want to talk? Try to convince her to use another instrument, and we will console her and send her over.

Guide

— We will try... She asks only that you apologize to Diane for her. Thank you and good night.

Carole

— If you have any more information on Patrick, will you let us know through Mario and his automatic writing?

Guide

— We certainly will. What beautiful work!

Over the years, the Spirit World often used little birds as messengers when they had something special for me. The next morning I was awakened early by the sound of a little bird that had somehow come in through the window, and was caught behind the short drapes. I gently pulled the curtain aside, and saw the most beautiful little bird I had ever seen. It was very small, and its feathers were several different colors, but the predominant color was yellow. The window was only open about a half inch, and I couldn't imagine it coming through that small a space, but somehow it had. It was very nervous, and I talked to it very softly and lovingly. Then I picked it up in my hand and opened the window wider to let it fly away. I sensed that it had been sent to thank me for the work we had done the night before, and I thanked God for this blessing.

Because the following Monday was our Canadian Thanksgiving, we waited until Tuesday to drive to the area to see what we could find. Bernard and Mario picked me up at 10:00 a.m., and we headed towards the Ontario border. Mario was to be our connection with the guides if we needed them, through his automatic writing.

The area she had mentioned was a few miles past the small city where the guides said she had lived. As we drove past, I couldn't help thinking about her, and wondering where she might have lived. But I kept my thoughts very low key. I knew from past experiences that it was very important not to tune into her energy too strongly, because she would feel the pull and would be drawn right back down into the earth's atmosphere; and the first thing she would do would be to head back to us.

As we reached the part of the country we were looking for, we left the highway and took the narrow road along the St. Lawrence River where all the homes and cottages were situated. We started searching for the driveways that might lead to the cottage which we had seen psychically. In Canada, everyone who has a summer home chooses Thanksgiving weekend to close it up for the winter months. As we drove several miles along this road, I realized that this was what had happened. Most of the driveways had a chain across them at the roadside entrance.

We started driving back very slowly, and decided to drive down all the driveways that did not have a chain. As we drove down the few that were accessible to us, none of them fit the picture each of us had in our minds. Some of them were a dead end, with an empty cottage which did not fit the description. Others were an empty lot on the water side. As we went down each narrow road my heart would beat faster, for we never knew what we would find at the end. One of them was about half a mile long and very narrow. Because it had rained, there were ruts about ten inches deep; and I really began to panic! I realized that because of the state of the road, it would be impossible for us to turn around and go back. I had visions of us arriving at the end of the road and seeing the van and the cottage, which were imprinted so deeply in my mind at that point! I could just imagine us arriving in their yard, and the three of them coming out to see what we were doing there. I heard myself saying that we had taken the wrong driveway! To my great joy and relief, we came out on a narrow back road, which took us back to the original one.

We didn't dare take a chance on going down the ones which had chains. If we had been caught, we would have had no excuse for trespassing, and might have gotten into some serious trouble. We asked the guides to help through Mario, and they did the best they could. The mother was resting, however, and if they wanted to get more information from her, they would have to ask her. This was a problem because, if they did, she would know that the story of the rescue was not true. She would be right back down here, bothering us once again.

I was praying for the little boy all the way home, asking God to come and get him. I felt like I was in a state of shock! I would rather see him over there with his mother than being brought up by murderers such as they were. I couldn't get the picture of his curly blond hair and sweet little face out of my mind. But then I had to bring myself back down to earth and remember the Spiritual teachings I shared with others, and the natural law of "cause and effect!" This means that *there is a reason for everything* that happens in the universe, and that somehow karma is being worked out in each experience.

Ten days later, a young detective from the Quebec Police Squad five miles from where I live showed up at my business office, asking to speak with me. The Ontario Provincial Police had transferred the file to him to interview me. I took the tape, and we went into a private office to talk. I explained briefly about my work and what a medium was, and then played the tape for him. He was very polite and friendly, and I didn't feel skepticism on his part; but he didn't have any answers either. When he left, I asked him what he would have done in my place. He only shrugged his shoulders!

Sometimes I would pick up bits and pieces about the young woman through my intuition. I felt that she had only moved to that town with her young son a few weeks before all this happened; and, because of her drug problem, had kept to herself. She had probably not made any friends, so when she disappeared, her neighbors thought that she had moved on as quickly as she had appeared. I watched the newspapers for a few months, looking for news of someone recovering the body of an unidentified young woman in the St. Lawrence River; but, remembering her telling us that they had "put her body in a bag and the bag in cement", it could have stayed at the bottom of the river for a long time.

Chapter Seven

BIZARRE PHENOMENA
IN MONTREAL NORTH

In August 1985, I received a call from Denise, a young woman who lived in the northern part of the city of Montreal. She had seen the programs I had done on the subject of soul rescue for Pierre Milot the year before, and had called him to ask for my phone number.

Denise had been having manifestations in the apartment she shared with her elderly mother and brother for the past three years. They had gotten much stronger during the last three weeks, and she decided she needed help. Although Denise was a person with many spiritual gifts, I felt immediately that she hadn't always used them the right way.

It had become so bad by the time Denise called me, that she and her mother were seeing what looked like astral human forms dressed in black. They were walking around the apartment, especially at night in the bedroom. The apartment smelled of sulfur, which is always an indication of *very negative entities*. The energy had gotten so negative that the plants all started to die; and the cats were really acting strangely, almost as if they were possessed at times. They finally had to move out altogether when articles started being physically projected around the apartment.

Until something could be done about the problem, they moved in with another brother.

Thursday was my day off from the business at that point in my life, and my soul rescue work in other areas of the Province was scheduled on that day. We made an appointment, and Denise was to meet me at the apartment. Because it might be too dangerous to do on my own, I called Tony Sheldon to make sure he was available. Tony worked with me on the tough cases, when I needed another medium to be the channel.

From the information I had received from Denise, I knew I would need additional people to help with the energy. Therese, who had worked with me before, and another spiritual friend were going to assist.

When we arrived, we immediately sensed the negative energy in the place. Tony and I walked into each room to "discern," and we felt that there were *several* entities present, not just one! Then, we sat down with the people concerned, and asked them to tell us about all the phenomena that had been happening. It is at this moment that I can separate "spirit phenomena" from their own imagination or fears!

From what Denise had told me, I knew that she had been dabbling in the occult for a long period of time. She thought that there was possibly some black magic being used against her by another member of her family, with whom she had not been on very good terms for a long while. She then told us that she could astral project herself to anywhere she wanted. Often she went to her aunt's house astrally, to find out what she could about her comings and goings. I told her that it was against natural and spiritual law to use her gifts for such purposes; and that the law of "cause and effect" would bring everything back to *her*. I now understood why all the negative entities were drawn to her, because "like attracts like!"

When we had the information we needed, we moved into a large bedroom. It had enough space for the four of them to sit facing Tony. We put our candles, incense and Holy Water on a small table.

Tony sat down in his chair and prepared to go into his trance state. I was standing behind him, ready for whatever would transpire. Sometimes the entities don't show their true colors until the guides have forced them into the channel, and then they manifest their discontent very strongly.

Tony's beautiful North American Indian guide came in to say an opening prayer in his native tongue. None of us understood, of course, but we bathed in the essence of this Spiritual Being. Understanding the words was unimportant. He then gave us some information on what was occurring in the apartment. When he was finished, they were ready to begin.

It didn't take very long for the spirit to control Tony's body. I knew that it was a male vibration, and he wasn't very happy about being there! Once we had the entity in the channel, I moved in front of Tony to be able to better communicate with the spirit. I stayed very close in case it suddenly decided to manifest violently, and I had to control him physically, to avoid endangering Tony's body. He didn't want to answer questions, and tried to ignore me most of the time. I finally provoked him a little, but still didn't get much reaction, except for his insisting he was not leaving! Finally I pretended anger, and told him he had to go; that he was dead, and had no business staying around bothering people. I told him to look towards the Light in front of him, and to move into it. I asked him if he could see it; and, if so, what color was it? He finally answered that he could see blue and purple lights, and they were very beautiful. I tried to convince him to move into it, he finally accepted and he was gone! I still felt that something strange was happening, because I had never done a rescue where the spirit was so low key. It was as if he were playing a game of some kind, for there were no emotions involved. He seemed to be saying what he knew I wanted to hear!

After our rescue was completed, we blessed each room with Holy Water. Then it was time for coffee in the kitchen. I always take advantage of this time to educate them as much as I can about the psychic. I advise them not to play around with it, because it can be dangerous. Everyone always has a million questions, and I try to answer as many as I can. It was late when we left, and I was happy to be heading home. I had an hour long drive ahead of me!

The next morning the phone rang. It was Denise, saying that after we left, things were worse than ever! She said that it was so bad that the cats had been thrown against the wall by unseen hands. They could hear the spirit swearing in a very raucous voice, telling them that they were not going to make him leave! Of course she had moved right back into her brother's house. I told her I could not go back again before the following Thursday; and if she wanted to wait, I would be there again. Not having any choice, she accepted.

The next week I was ready once again, but I knew that it would be a much harder task! I asked Frank Beauchamp and Pauline Rainville to assist. Frank is portly, and I knew he would have the strength to help me if there were a need for physical restraint.

On arriving, Tony's eyes roamed from left to right. I knew he was discerning, although the physical eyes are not used for this purpose. Psychic energy is used to feel the different vibrations in the place. It tells us if something is positive or negative, and to what degree. He looked at me and said, "My God, Carole, it's going to be rough here tonight!" I answered that it would be alright, for we had two extra people to help. After listening to what had transpired over the past week, we decided to move our temporary seance room into a very wide area that resembled a hall, connecting all the rooms in the apartment. We put a table in the middle and lit extra candles and incense; the Holy Water was ready. We brought chairs from the kitchen and put them around the table, and I positioned my people where they would be the most efficient for the work each would be doing.

Frank sat a little in front and to the left of Tony, so he would be close if I needed his help. I took off my shoes, as working in my bare feet always makes me feel grounded in my work, in case I have to move fast. Tony's guide came in for the opening prayer, and then we were ready to begin.

It took a few minutes, for the spirit had decided he wasn't coming through, no matter how much I coaxed him. Finally the guides forced him in, which didn't please him at all! He came in protesting violently, both verbally and physically, and I quickly protected Tony's body by moving to his side and putting my arms around him. With Frank's help, we physically held him in the chair. He was thrashing around so violently that the chair was rocking from left to right and back to front. Everything happened so fast, that I didn't realize how close and vulnerable my bare feet were. In one of his violent movements, he brought the leg of the chair smashing down onto my right foot. The chair was heavy and made of chrome, with a large round metal pad under each leg. As he brought it down with all of his force, the pain was excruciating. The whole top of my foot turned blue instantly, and I was sure my foot was broken! I don't think he did it intentionally; my foot just happened to be in the way. I had to lift the chair up to get my foot out, but knew that I had no time to think of the pain.

Once he finally started to talk, everything was negative! No matter how I tried to convince him, there was no way he was leaving the apartment. After about half an hour of discussion, he was still adamant; he was not going anywhere! I searched my brain for another plot I could use, possibly to trick him if need be, for I knew that every spirit had a vulnerable spot. I had to keep trying until I found it. I finally thought of asking him if he wanted to see his family. He became very emotional and angry, and said that his wife had left him. He wanted nothing to do with her, but I knew I had touched a sensitive spot. I asked him, "Wouldn't you like to see your children?" Instantly his face changed, and he started to break down. A few tears started to flow, and I knew that I had him! But he was still not ready to give in and said very angrily, "No! They turned their backs on me and wouldn't have anything to do with me!" I pretended that I was disgusted with him and said loudly, "I don't blame them for doing that! If you were as mean to your children as you are to the people in this house, you certainly couldn't have given them the love they needed; and you didn't deserve their love." But I could see there was still a lot of resentment, and he was far from being ready to forgive. I was getting impatient and asked him, "Who do you want to see in your family?" He answered, "My brother."

At that point he started to scream and writhe in his chair, and sobbed that he was in pain! I asked him where, and he said "all over my body." I was feeling the symptoms of someone who had died from a generalized cancer in my own body, but I wasn't sure if this was the cause of his death, or if the guides had projected the pain to him to oblige him to leave. I took advantage of this pain to force him out, and told him to look at the Light in front of him. I explained that he would see his brother there, for he had come to get him. I warned him very strongly: "Don't you come back down here. You stay with your brother because, if you do come back, you will feel the same pain again!" He looked as if he were suffering so much physically, that he no longer had any desire to stay. Suddenly he asked for a crucifix, and I took the one from the table and handed it to him. He kissed it and started saying the Lord's Prayer, with his head bowed. Each of us said it aloud with him; and when he was finished, Tony's body suddenly became very limp. The crucifix clattered to the floor as the spirit finally left.

When we were through, my foot was still throbbing from the pain; but I had to go with Tony and Therese to bless the four corners of each room with the candles and the Holy Water. I did this walking only on my heel, and we found a few spirits in the bathroom, and convinced them telepathically to leave. We often find some in the bathrooms, because water and the copper pipes seem to be a good conduit to help the spirits to manifest.

As we came back through the room where we had held the seance, I stood by the table to discern. All of a sudden I felt very weak, and my solar plexus began to vibrate strongly. I had never felt such a strange vibration before, and looked around to see where it was coming from. Immediately, in the corner across from me, I saw the Holy Mother Mary descending into the room. She was dressed in a beautiful blue and white gown with a gold sash. The whole scene was just so powerful, and my body was still vibrating very strongly. I felt weak from the emotions, and I started to sob, and fell into a chair which was just behind me. She gently glided over to me and went down on her knees, putting both of her hands on my foot that was injured, as if she were doing "the laying on of hands!" As she did this, the color of the huge bruise on my foot became lighter and lighter. Suddenly it disappeared, along with the pain!

Through my sobs, I tried to explain to the others in the room what was happening. They told me they sensed the powerful vibration, but could not physically see her. However, they could see the color of my foot changing. When Mother Mary was finished, she stood up and looked at me with so much love. It was like nothing I had ever felt before! She then glided back to the same corner, reached into the wide sleeve of her gown, and produced some beautiful roses. She threw them to the other people in the room who had helped me, and slowly ascended.

After she left, the bruise on my foot came back. It was a dark purple color, but the pain had completely disappeared! I felt that she had left the color as proof of the injury. I took a few minutes to balance my emotions, and we continued the job of discerning the rest of the house. As we got to one of the bedrooms, Frank felt a slight breeze coming from the closet. This is often an indication of the presence of spirits. We checked for other possibilities, and could find absolutely no explanation for this; so we went into an altered state of consciousness, to try to detect the reason for this phenomenon.

We could psychically see a passageway that led to what looked like a large hole that went straight down deep into the earth. This pit was full of souls that were burning, and crying out for help. Frank and I were a little shocked. It reminded me of a soul rescue I did in one of my classes a few years before, when a woman came through Rose. When I finished the rescue, she explained that she had been in a place like this: a pit where a huge fire was burning, and everyone was suffering! When she realized she was free, she sobbed "please go and help the others! There are thousands of people burning in that big hole, and they don't know how to get out! Please! Please! Go and help them!" I was angry, because I knew these souls found themselves in the situation in which they *expected* to find themselves, having heard all of their life about the "hell" that awaited them because of their "sins"; therefore, after "death", there was nothing else they *could* find!

As we stood there wondering about the best way to help them, I psychically saw a stairway building up on the left side of the closet. As it got higher, I saw Jesus descending; He came nearly to the bottom and held out His right hand. I heard Him say with a great deal of love, "Those of you who are ready to leave must come to me; I can go no further, because you still have "free will"!" One by one they started floating up out of the pit of fire, and He was waiting for them.

We watched for a few minutes, fascinated, as they floated up one by one to accept the loving hand that was held out to them. It was getting late, so we went to the kitchen for a cup of coffee, giving Jesus time to finish his task. When we went back later, all seemed to be finished. The energy in the room was much lighter, and the cool breeze was no longer coming from the closet. We blessed the room with Holy Water, and knew that there was no more we could do.

The next morning, as I walked down the three steps that led to our business office from our house, one of our secretaries turned with a smile to say good morning. Suddenly, the look on Johanne's face turned to shock as she noticed the huge purple bruise covering the whole top of my foot! I laughed at the look on her face, and started sharing with her and Mireille, our other wonderful secretary who had been with us for fifteen years, my experience of the night before, and the fact that the foot was completely free of pain. She couldn't believe that I was able to walk on a foot that looked the way mine did! My brother Don, from Ottawa, came to visit me eight days later. I told him about the experience, and showed him my foot, which still had the bruise over three quarters of the instep, although it had lightened a little. He asked if I had taken a picture of it when it happened. I hadn't thought of it, but went and got my camera. The photo came out clearly and is in my files. At no time after I received the healing from Mother Mary did I feel pain of any kind. This to me was a true miracle!

Learning from Pauline that she did tarot cards and could read the crystal ball, Denise called her a week later and asked her to come over and bring it with her. When they arrived in front of the apartment, both she and Frank felt very uneasy. Pauline's intuition told her not to take the crystal ball into the apartment, so she left it in the car. When they went in and Denise heard that they had not brought it, she became very angry and was verbally abusive, so they left.

I have spent a lot of time over the years helping people with problems such as these, and I try to educate them as to the dangers of playing with the occult when they have no experience, and do not know how to protect themselves. I will go back a second time if need be, when I feel that the people involved have learned their lesson. If they want to take courses to develop their own gifts so that they may understand more, I will direct them to the best teachers available for their needs; but, if I see that they have drawn these negative entities to themselves because they enjoy the danger, I tell them "don't call me a third time. If you get yourself into trouble again, you just get yourself out of it!"

Chapter Eight

MY FIRST MEETING WITH BETTY

In March of 1984, I received a call from Therese. Her friend Betty was having a bad problem, and she needed me to visit her home in a suburb of Montreal. Betty was a lovely lady in her forties, who had recently started living on her own.

Tony and Therese met me there. Betty explained that there were some strange things happening, mostly in the basement, which was finished as a second living room and a sauna bath. Although she hadn't really started on her spiritual pathway at that moment, Betty was very sensitive to energies. Her cat started refusing to go down to the basement, and the door at the top of the stairs kept opening by itself, without reason. When Betty had to go down, she felt a cold chill. The hair would stand up on her arms, and she would feel a shiver all over her body. She felt that there was something very negative down there. She had been referred to another medium; however, on opening the door at the top of the basement stairs, the medium refused to go any further, explaining it was *too bad* for her to undertake. I must state here that many mediums do rescue work, helping the lost souls go to the Light, but not many want to take on a task that can consist of a very negative or sometimes called "evil" spirit. I don't blame them, for you never know what to expect when you start a case. If there is the least bit of fear, this only tends to help the spirit manifest more strongly; they nourish themselves through other peoples emotional energy. So it's always best to know our own limits. Working above these limits might have drastic consequences, marking a person for life with fear, and preventing him from continuing on his spiritual pathway. This is why it is important, when working on a strong case, to have only two or three people we can depend on for the energy, prayers and Light, and who are very compatible with us.

Tony and I both felt the negativity the moment we walked through the front door. For my part, negativity always manifests itself with a sharp pain at the back of my head. This does not necessarily mean spirits; it can mean negativity in general, as it can happen when I am standing in line at a grocery store. I will turn around to see who it is coming from and project the Light to them! With the spirits, it's always the hair standing up on my arms; sometimes I feel as if the hair on my head is going to stand up straight, along with a cold chill all over my body. We went down to the basement, for we felt that this was their favorite place, the spot where they came in and out of the house.

We went back upstairs and decided to hold our seance in the kitchen, so we set up the chairs, and placed the candles, crucifix and Holy Water on the table.

Tony's Indian guide and protector during his work, Chief Running Bear, was the first to come through. He started with a short prayer in his own native tongue and then explained what was happening: "We are gathered here for a cause of Light! I have here a distressed soul. I ask you to join with me in surrounding this soul, this being, in Light, for he is in need of much Light and Love. If you are in need of strength, call upon your Great White Spirit, God. Call upon your own higher selves. Call upon your Teachers and loved ones."

Carole

— Is there danger for the instrument?

Guide

— None.

Carole

— Is this the spirit who has been in this house several times?

Guide

— There are a multitude of spirits around; one who is greater, but more than one. He has been influenced, and has influenced many and much that has happened.

Carole

— Is this soul very evil or simply confused?

Guide

— Evil...? He is negative, let's just keep the word "negative", or evilness if you must...what can we say...it is there, yes, but I believe that his Creator is greater, and he shall be able to be in touch with the Light.

Carole

— Thank You.

———————

He came through immediately, manifesting very strongly and noisily; pounding his feet on the floor and rocking the chair from side to side. I was prepared for any eventuality because I didn't want any harm done to Tony's physical body. I kept inviting him to come through over and over again, while he kept banging and jerking back and forth. His manner of speaking was very aggressive during most of the dialogue, often shouting!

Carole

— It's alright, come on through... Quiet down now...We want to talk to you. Can you tell us your name? We want to help you; we know you're not happy where you are! You **can't** be happy where you are. Can you tell me about yourself? We're here to help you; just relax and take it easy. Come on through...You've been living in darkness for a long time now. We want to help you go to the Light. We want to help you leave this place.

Spirit

– **No!**

Carole

– Yes, you have to leave! You have to go on your path!

Spirit

– **No!**

Carole

– God Is calling you and you have to go on your pathway; you have to go into the Light.

Spirit

– **God! No!**

Carole

– Why are you staying here in this house?

Spirit

– **My Place!**

Carole

– This is not your place; did you ever live in this house?

Spirit

– No! I chose this place!

Carole

– Why did you choose this place?

Spirit

– Feels Good!

Carole

– But it's not your place, you'll have to go to another place. It doesn't belong to you; this house belongs to God. You'll have to go and find another place.

Spirit

– No! My Place!

Carole

- You're not happy here are you? Have you ever known happiness?

Spirit

- HUH! WHAT IS HAPPINESS?

Carole

- Happiness is being with God, finding love! Have you ever had love? Ever known love?

Spirit

- LOVE! YOU DON'T KNOW! HAPPINESS! THEY DON'T EXIST!

Carole

- Do you remember your name? Tell me your name.

Spirit

- (Raucous Laugh) NO!

Carole

- You don't remember or you're not going to tell me?

Spirit

- I'M NOT GOING TO TELL YOU!

Carole

- It doesn't matter; I like you anyway. Wouldn't you like to know love and feel love?

Spirit

- WHAT IS LOVE?

Carole

- Love is a beautiful feeling.

Spirit

- IT'S NOT POWER!

Carole

- There's nothing more powerful than love.

Spirit

- IT'S NOT **REAL** POWER!

Carole

- *Divine love is real power.*

Spirit
 – DIVINE LOVE!... DIVINE LOVE!... WHO IS GOD?
 WHAT IS GOD?
Carole
 – What do you think it is?
Spirit
 – (Laughter) A NONEXISTENT FORCE.
Carole
 – God does exist.
Spirit
 – NO! YOU DELUDE!
Carole
 – No I don't! Divine love exists and God exists!
Spirit
 – WHERE?
Carole
 – I can send you to a place where you can find Him.
Spirit
 – (Raucous Laughter) THEN I WON'T BE *HERE!*
Carole
 – You won't want to be here after you have found Him.
Spirit
 – SHOW ME FIRST!
Carole
 – O.K. , I'll put you into the Light!
Spirit
 – *NO YOU WON'T!* WHAT LIGHT?
Carole
 – See here right beside you, this is a beautiful big Light.
 It's like an elevator! You step into this Light and you can
 go up and find love. If you don't like it, you can come
 back down again!
Spirit
 – NO! YOU WANT ME TO LEAVE!

Carole

 – I want you to find happiness! I want you to find the Light; you won't find it here.

Spirit

 – I WON'T FIND IT ANYWHERE!

Carole

 – Yes, you will if you do as I say! You will find the Light.

Spirit

 – NO I WON'T!

Carole

 – You won't if you don't try it. Do you want to try it?

Spirit

 – NOT REALLY!

Carole

 – You should try it; you must get tired of staying here all the time. It must be very boring!

Spirit

 – I DON'T STAY IN THIS HOUSE; I COME IN AND OUT!

Carole

 – Just the same, you're still in the darkness all the time.

Spirit

 – I KNOW MY WAY!

Carole

 – Imagine the beauty you could see if it were always Light! You're surely not seeing any beauty in that darkness; you're only seeing darkness and despair!

Spirit

 – DARKNESS AND DESPAIR! TERRIBLE THINGS!

Carole

 – If you went into the Light, you could help people like you, who are in darkness and despair now.

Spirit

 – I HAVE MY FRIENDS.

Carole
- Take them with you; take them all into the Light with you. Would you do something for me?

Spirit
- POSSIBLY.

Carole
- Try to go into the Light and see what is up there! If you're not happy, you can come back and tell me.

Spirit
- WHAT'S IN IT FOR ME?

Carole
- Happiness.

Spirit
- WHAT IS HAPPINESS? I WANT SOMETHING CONCRETE!

Carole
- What do you want concrete?

Spirit
- WHAT IS THERE?

Carole
- All I can give you is happiness and love.

Spirit
- IT'S NOT CONCRETE.

Carole
- But you're a spirit now, you don't need anything concrete.

Spirit
- SPIRIT IS LIFE, YOU SHOULD KNOW THAT!

Carole
- Yes, but you don't have a physical body anymore, so you don't need concrete things; you need Light and love to go on your soul path.

Spirit
- I NEED TO EXIST!

Carole

— Yes, you will continue to exist on a higher plane once you get into the Light, and then you can really find happiness. Try It for me! Go up and you will meet some people, and you'll see beautiful things.

Spirit

— WHAT LIGHT?

Carole

— The Light right here beside you; you just have to go in.

Spirit

— IT'S NOT BIG ENOUGH!

Carole

— I'll make it bigger then! You see, it's expanding.

Spirit

— WHO IS THIS WHO EXPANDS IT? THERE IS SOMEBODY RIGHT THERE!

Carole

— (It Is Tony's Indian Guide). It is a friend of ours who is helping. You can see more already, can't you? Is it much larger now?

Spirit

— TELL THIS PERSON TO GO!

Carole

— I will tell him to move away, but he's trying to help you also. He wants to help you move into the Light.

Spirit

— THIS IS MY PLACE!

Carole

— (He starts to manifest strongly.) I can't go up there, and I would like you to find out what's up there for me. You're only going to find happiness in the Light; you won't find it where you are now. Step out of the darkness and into the Light. You're going to feel yourself moving upward; and as you do, you'll find the Light getting brighter and brighter! They're all Light Beings; not the dark beings you've been with down here.

Spirit

— THEY SURROUND ME... THEY SURROUND ME...

Carole

— Up you go! You're going to find happiness, you're going to find God there, and you'll know that He loves you. Calm down! Move very slowly!

Spirit

— THEY SURROUND ME... THEY SURROUND ME...

Carole

— Keep moving up; you're coming out of the darkness now, and into the Light. You may find some members of your family there.

Spirit

— (Almost a scream) No! THEY KILLED ME!

Carole

— Well, they're sorry now!

Spirit

— No!

Carole

— O.K., then they won't be there! You'll have to move slowly when you get there, because you're not used to the Light. Go slowly sweetheart, there are a lot of people around to help you. Do you see the Light now? Just relax and let the Light penetrate you. (He's very agitated.) Go towards Divine Light! Let go of the darkness and go towards the Light! Release all the darkness and leave it behind you. Go to the Light; God is waiting for you.

Spirit

— No, HE IS THERE!

Carole

— Who is He?

Spirit

 —*HE* IS THERE!

Carole

 — Who is it? (He is near tears.)

Spirit

 — GREGORY!

Carole

 — Who is Gregory?

Spirit

 — ST. GREGORY! I KNOW HIM; HE IS MY BROTHER!

Carole

 — He is there to help you! He is your brother? He works
   for God, doesn't he?

Spirit

 — HE WORKS FOR THE LORD!

Carole

 — He's come to help and to prove to you that the Lord does
   exist.

Spirit

 —*I KNOW THAT!*

Carole

 — You've always known that, but you refused to accept it.
   Is he talking to you?

Spirit

 — HE'S STANDING THERE.

Carole

 — He's waiting to help you; he wants to take you into the
   Light! Ask him to approach you, tell him that you want
   to talk to him.

Spirit

 — HE WILL WAIT!

Carole

 — He will wait until you are ready because you have to do
   it. Tell him that you want to go with him... that you want

to see the Lord, and that you want the Lord's Blessing on you to help you go into this Light. Go with him, love, go with him! Lord have mercy on this child of yours who has taken the wrong path, but now wants to return to the path of righteousness. (He starts to sob and asks for a Crucifix, which I give him.) You have Jesus with you. (He starts to pray softly, asking God to have mercy on his soul.) God has forgiven you and invites you to go into his Kingdom with him; you have to accept, no one can force you, but you will find happiness there! God Bless You! We love you!

Spirit

– I WAS A GOD ONCE; I WAS ONCE A PRIEST. I BLESS YOU!

Carole

– We thank you for your blessing and now you have found the right path again.

Spirit

– MAY GOD'S LOVE WATCH OVER YOU!

Carole

– And also over you.

Spirit

– I HOPE!

Carole

– God is forgiveness, God is love, God is compassion.

Spirit

– GOD IS WHAT HE IS.

Carole

– Yes, He is beautiful! Whenever you are ready, you can just leave the body and go with St. Gregory.

He left gently without saying another word. Running Bear came back in saying we needed more energy. When a spirit comes through with as much emotion as this one did, it takes a lot out of the medium; and they have to re-balance the emotional body.

Running Bear: "I wish to open the Light and allow those who are left to go through. I want you to energize the room with Light; and, if possible illumine another candle beside the other one. Bring forth your blessing and prayers so that those who are left may journey into the Light. God's love surrounds us always. (He says a prayer in his native tongue.)

Within a few minutes, another spirit had taken over Tony's body; and we were ready to go to work again! He came in and looked around at everyone. I greeted him:

Carole

  — Hello!

Spirit

  — I AM BRUNO. I WISH TO FIND SOMEONE!

Carole

  — Who are you looking for, Bruno?

Spirit

  — HE WHO WAS HERE! WE WISH TO FIND BRUNO!

Carole

  — Are you Bruno?

Spirit

  — WE ARE ALL BRUNOS.

Carole

    — I know where he is. Did you see the Light when he went up awhile ago?

Spirit

  — WE WISH TO FIND HIM. WHERE IS BRUNO?

Carole

    — He's gone into the Light right beside you, and he waits for you up there!

Spirit
   – WE WANT TO GO NOW! WHAT LIES THERE?

Carole
   – The Light of God lies there. God is Divine Love.

Spirit
   – GOD IS AS HE IS!

Carole
   – Bruno went up and he told us to tell all of you to follow
     him.

Spirit
   – BRUNO WOULD NOT LEAVE! YOU LIE!

Carole
   – You go up and see if he isn't there, and you come back
     and tell me if I am lying! They're all up there, and he
     said to tell you all to follow him up.

Spirit
   – WE WILL GO, BUT WE SHALL RETURN IF HE SHOULD
     NOT BE THERE!

Carole
   – He will be there waiting for you. How many are there
     of you?

Spirit
   – A NUMBER OF US.

Carole
   – He wants you all to go together into the elevator.

Spirit
   – WE SHALL GO! WHO IS THERE? THERE ARE BEINGS;
     WHO ARE THEY?

Carole
   – They are Beings of Light.

Spirit
   – WHAT IS LIGHT? (Laughter) LIGHT IS THE ABSENCE
     OF DARKNESS.

Carole

   – Light is beauty and happiness. What is darkness?

Spirit

   – DARKNESS IS COMFORT.

Carole

   – Once you have felt the Light you won't want any more darkness.

Spirit

   – WE SHALL SEE!

Carole

   – O.K., take everyone with you! (He pauses for a couple of minutes and I ask what is happening.) Are you in now?

Spirit

   – I'M THINKING! I THINK THESE PEOPLE HERE SHOULD LET US GO IN WITHOUT THEIR BEING THERE. (He's talking about the guides he sees around the Light.)

Carole

   – ***Just get in and go up!***

Spirit

   – ALRIGHT!

Carole

   – I'm pushing the button and you're moving up. How many are you in the elevator?

Spirit

   – THE NUMBER IS SEVEN.

Carole

   – Is that all there were here in the house?

Spirit

   – THERE WERE EIGHT OF US WITH BRUNO.

Carole

   – Keep going up; he will be there to meet you. Let me know when it stops.

Spirit

    — WHERE IS YOUR LIGHT?

Carole

    — It is still there; can you feel it warming you?

Spirit

    — IT IS DIFFERENT; FROM DARKNESS UNTO LIGHT! IT HAS STOPPED.

Carole

    — The door is going to open and you will see Bruno there and also other people who want to help you.

Spirit

    — *I HOPE SO!*

Carole

    — He's there; Do you see him? He's surrounded with Light!

Spirit

    — HE WAS HERE!

Carole

    — Where has he gone? He left someone to take care of you; who is it?

Spirit

    — HE WAS HERE, YES! *HIS BROTHER! HIS BROTHER!* (He begins to get very emotional.)

Carole

    — O.K. Go with his brother, because he met him also. Do you feel the beauty around you?

Spirit

    — IT IS DIFFERENT!

Carole

    — Yes, it surely is different... Have confidence...

Spirit:...

    — IN THE LORD MY GOD (Laughs). OH, WHAT WE HAVE DONE! WE LEFT LIGHT TO GO INTO DARKNESS, AND FROM DARKNESS INTO LIGHT!

Carole

   – Yes, and now you're home again!

Spirit

   – THE CYCLE CONTINUES.

Carole

   – No, it shouldn't continue; now you must stay in the Light. You have to go in the Light, not go back to darkness again.

Spirit

   – WE SHALL SEE!

Carole

   – It depends on you!

Spirit

   – IT DEPENDS ON MANY THINGS.

Carole

   – Yes, but it depends mostly on you; finding love...

Spirit

   – ...AND LIGHT AND HAPPINESS AND JOY... PRAISE BE TO THE LORD JESUS CHRIST OUR SAVIOR; I'VE SAID THOSE WORDS MANY TIMES! THE LORD IS WITH US!

Carole

   – He is *Now!*

Spirit

   – THE LORD..., ST. GREGORY!

Carole

   – Are you out of the elevator now?

Spirit

   – I AM PONDERING!

Carole

   – They will take you to find Bruno; they know where he is.

Spirit

   – WE ARE WAITING FOR A SIGN!

Carole

— They will give you the sign. It's much better to live in the Light than the darkness.

Spirit

— IT'S BETTER TO BE COMFORTABLE!

Carole

— Comfortable isn't anything at all, when you can have love, Light and joy in your life. Go with St. Gregory!

Spirit

— I WISH TO WAIT A MINUTE.

Carole

— Tell the others to go with you.

Spirit

— THEY SHALL FOLLOW. THERE IS ONE I AM WAITING FOR!

Carole

— Can you hear the beautiful music playing there?

Spirit

— *I SEE THE GOLDEN DAWN!*

Carole

— Beautiful...

Spirit

— *AND HE COMES! PRAISE BE TO YOU, LORD JESUS CHRIST! I SHALL GO NOW!*

Carole

— God Bless you!

Spirit

— AND YOU ALSO.

Carole

— Don't go back into the darkness now, stay in the Light! Is it Bruno who is there?

Spirit

— *IT IS GOD! LORD JESUS IS REAL!* LORD, OUR HEAVENLY SAVIOR TOUCHES EACH ONE OF YOU,

AND YOU SHALL FIND EACH OF YOU RECEIVING A
GIFT FROM HIM IN DUE COURSE. EVEN THOUGH I
WALK IN THE SHADOW OF DEATH, I WILL FEAR NO
EVIL, (and he was gone).

Running Bear came back in to tell us what they wanted
us to do next: "WE SHALL NOW MOVE UPON EACH FLOOR
FROM CORNER TO CORNER WITH FIRE AND WATER, ANOINT-
ING THE HOUSE, BRINGING DOWN THE LORD'S BLESSINGS,
REMOVING ALL NEGATIVITY THAT RESIDES, AND SEALING
THIS ABODE AGAINST ALL NEWCOMERS. I ASK YOU TO
CARRY THE WATER, THE INCENSE, THE CANDLES AND THE
CRUCIFIX, FOUR THINGS FOR FOUR PEOPLE; AND WE SHALL
INVOKE THE PRAYERS OF GOD UPON THIS HOUSE, FOR HIS
POWERS HAVE ENTERED IN HERE AND TOUCHED US ALL.
THEREFORE THIS HOUSE IS NOW A HOLY PLACE, HOLY
UNTO THE LORD OUR HEAVENLY FATHER, SACRED
GROUND IN WHICH TO PRAY. PRAISE BE TO YOU LORD
JESUS CHRIST! AMEN."

We were all very moved by this soul rescue, for I knew
that at least the first and second had been Catholic priests
in their last lifetimes. Something had happened at some
point, and the first one had fallen from Grace; he had refused
to go to the Light when he passed to spirit. As I have
mentioned, "like attracts like," and he had surrounded himself with a group of like thinkers in the fourth dimension,
but he was definitely their leader. They had been drawn to
that particular house because someone had lived there for
many years who was a Minister of a church with an attitude
problem. He had the same negative way of thinking, and
they felt comfortable.

We wanted to do a little research on St. Gregory and found that there had been two Saints with the same name. What was very interesting to us was the fact that one of them had founded a congregation in France whose members were called the "Brunants". Therefore, when the second spirit said, "We are all Brunos," I sensed that they had all been priests at some time in their lives, and had banded together on the other side because they had something in common. That was why they felt "comfortable".

The beautiful vibrations which have stayed in Betty's house since that night seven years ago leave me with no doubt that her home was specially blessed, and so was she. She is a very beautiful soul, and has come a long way on her spiritual path since that night. I feel very blessed to have her as one of my dearest friends, always there to give me encouragement and a loving push when I get discouraged and doubt myself, especially after the last three years of soul growth we "Aries" went through. No matter where I was, I had only to pick up the phone and hear her loving voice, and I had things back in perspective in a few minutes. Being the "double Virgo" she is, it wouldn't take long for me to get my two feet back on the ground!

Chapter Nine

SOUL RESCUE CASES
DONE ON TELEVISION

One morning as I got up, not even thinking of my book at that moment, the picture of the video tape on which I had done some cases for Pierre Milot on his parapsychology program back in 1984, suddenly popped into my mind. This is the way Spirit works when they want to impress us with some idea they think is worthwhile. They can always reach us more easily on awakening, when our minds are still quiet from a good night's sleep, before we start to fill it up again with all of the clutter of our daily thoughts. I hadn't watched this video tape in years. After seeing it again, I knew they were right; this had been a very important program. I hadn't planned on writing a chapter on my soul rescue experiences on radio and television; but it had brought Pierre so much response from his viewers, and I knew it should be shared.

Two previous hour long programs I had done for Pierre had been very popular, one on soul rescue – with the telephone lines opened to the viewers for calls for the last half hour, and one on François and his mother. Pierre asked if it would be possible to do a third program with one of my mediums in a trance state, so that the viewers could see soul rescue for themselves. I didn't know if we could, because we would be working in a completely different energy; but, because it would be filmed beforehand, I was ready to try. From the other programs I had done, I knew that the crew he worked with were at least open to psychic phenomena. Some of them had even shared their personal experiences in this field with me. It is very important for the success of research in any branch of phenomena, whether it be mediumship, healing, physical phenomena, etc., that there not be people present that are very negative towards the subject. They must at least be open-minded, for their negativity can sometimes counteract what we are trying to do.

Pierre started the program with a recapitulation of soul rescue work for the benefit of the viewers who might have missed the first show I did on the subject. I explained that most of my cases were done in my weekly classes through my mediums, whom I had developed over a period of weeks and months. It is very easy to develop those who, from past life experiences, have mediumship potential very close to the surface of their beings. Often they have used it since they were children, not understanding what it was. It is even easier if there is no fear involved, for they need to have complete trust in the person who is helping them develop. They must feel that, no matter what happens, they know their teacher can handle it and they are never in danger.

I then explained that these were souls who had been directed to us for help. Most of them had passed to the Spirit World without knowing it, and did not realize they were dead. Others were still attached to the earth plane through their material sense, or their family. Pierre then gave the example:

Pierre

– I get into my car on a Friday afternoon. It's a sunny day, I'm happy that my week is finished, and everything is fine in my life! I'm driving along the highway, and suddenly in a curve I lose control of the car; and I am killed instantly. I am not a person who has ever really thought about death or had any interest in the afterlife, and suddenly I find myself on the other side; I don't know that I am dead. Is that what you are saying? What happens then?

Carole

– It depends on the evolution of your soul. If the soul was not ready, and consciously and physically you didn't expect to die, you wander on the astral plane, the new dimension you have gone into. You are now in your astral body, which is a replica of your physical body. Therefore you think everything is still the same, as often the shock of the accident has wiped it completely out of your mind. You go home, you try to talk to your family, and you wonder why they are ignoring you! Sometimes you try to touch them, and your hand goes right through them. You get very upset, not understanding why they are acting this way. Sometimes you find yourself in complete darkness.

Pierre

– The people who are watching us are probably asking themselves why it happens this way. One thing we need to explain, and that most people don't understand, is that when we pass over, we remain exactly the person we were; I am still Pierre Milot and you are still Carole Langlois, which means that what we love, what we hate, our fears, the emotions which are particular to each of us, etc., remain exactly the same. The only difference is that we no longer have a physical body!

Carole

– Yes, that is right.

Pierre

> – It must be very traumatic for the person. These are the people whom you help through the intervention of a medium?

Carole

> – Yes. They are directed to me by spirit helpers, whose task is to help these souls. When they come to me, they are ready to be liberated, even though they sometimes don't know it. Often they don't understand what they are doing there themselves; but on some level of their consciousness, they are there because they are ready to accept the Light. Without really knowing it, they are accepting their death. Otherwise, the spirit helpers could not intervene because they still have "free will". But there are special cases that the Guides send us. I remember one that was a father of four young boys. While he was working, he had fallen from the tenth floor of a high rise building under construction. He fell head first onto a small stove which was burning on the ground. He came in screaming, with his arms up over his face. He sobbed that he was blind, and that his eyes were burning! I tried to convince him to release, and go to the Light, but he said he couldn't leave his four sons. I was finally able to talk him into leaving by telling him that he could help his children a lot more from over there, and he accepted. The guides came in and told us that they had been trying for ten years, through different groups, to rescue him; but it had never worked. They said that the little boys had loved their father very much and after his death they continually invoked his help. This had kept him earthbound.

Pierre

> – Does this mean that if my wife or my mother dies, and emotionally I don't accept this, that I can prevent them from advancing?

Carole
- That's right. They have to stay around to help the family
  through the period of mourning because of the love connection, but it hinders their own evolution. What we should
  do is to pray for them, and send them Light and love,
  and tell them to continue on their pathway. Sometimes
  there is a sense of guilt because of the things we did or
  didn't do, or the things we didn't say, and wish we had!
  We are usually the ones who need them for some reason
  or other. Often a very insecure person will have a loved
  one taken from him, so that he may be able to acquire
  the soul growth needed, by being obliged to take responsibility for himself, possibly for the first time in his life.

Pierre
- Can you explain a little about what we are going to be
  viewing?

Carole
- Yes. I brought one of my mediums, Rose, whom I developed in one of my classes. In fact she fell into a deep
  trance state the first time she sat in a circle in a beginners
  course, which means that her mediumship potential was
  very close to the surface. She is one of the best mediums
  I have found for soul rescue work, because she goes into
  a very deep state, and has no knowledge of what is
  transpiring through her. In fact, she has to listen to the
  tape the next day to find out what happened. Soul rescue
  can be done in many ways:

  > The medium can be in anything from an altered
  > state of consciousness, where he or she is describing
  > what they are seeing, and repeating what they are
  > hearing mentally, to a very deep state. In this state,
  > their consciousness leaves their physical body, and is
  > usually taken to the other side by their guide, where

it is given knowledge, although they don't remember on returning. The physical body can be used as a channel by spirit, for the time needed to get the task done. Of course our spiritual guides are always working with us during this period, more or less controlling the whole seance from their side. Each medium has a spiritual guide who is his "Doorkeeper", who always protects their body and serves as control, and decides who will be allowed to use it during the owner's absence. They will never let a channel's body be taxed to the limit. When they see that the energy is getting low, they will re-energize the physical body, bringing them out of their trance. The medium returns feeling relaxed, as if they are awakening from a wonderful night of sleep.

Pierre

– If a spirit doesn't want to leave her body, her guide will force it out?

Carole

– They will try, but sometimes we have to do it from our side; because there is a limit to what the guides can do when working with physical energy. They depend on us to do our part of the work, and help us the best they can; but remember, we are always working with energies. If you look at the rare exorcisms the church does, it sometimes takes them several days of continual work to get the diabolical spirits to leave.

Pierre

– What is your part in the work? Do you serve as guide to the spirit who comes through?

Carole

– Yes, I talk to them, and convince them to leave by accepting to go to the Light. I want to explain that I don't see "death" the same way an ordinary person does. The people who are watching us tonight may think that I work in a strange way, because sometimes I laugh with the spirit. I have to get into the atmosphere, and be part of whatever they *think* is happening around them. I do this to gain their confidence in order to do my task properly. If the spirit doesn't know it has died, I don't tell them. I leave that to the guides who receive them once they have gone into the Light. When a spirit is permitted to temporarily occupy the physical body of a medium, it doesn't really know what is happening! It only knows that it has finally found a way to express itself verbally. Therefore, it comes in speaking the same way it did before passing. It can be very emotional, crying and sobbing; or it can be very angry, using every swear word it can think of, if they were a person whose vocabulary contained a lot of these words, especially if they passed while in a drugged state. Sometimes we have to laugh in spite of what is happening, because Rose has a very expressive face which makes us laugh when she is in a normal state. I remember one spirit coming in and looking around the circle at every face, trying to recognize where he was. He was shocked to find himself sitting with a group of strangers! He became upset and asked what he was doing at a party in his long underwear. He bent over and grabbed his behind and said, "Is my back door closed, at least?" Needless to say, we all burst into laughter! I asked him what he remembered, and he said he had gotten ready for bed, and was sitting in his rocking chair in his long johns. After a short discussion, he remembered that he had felt a pain in his chest, and it only took a moment for him to realize that he must have died. It didn't take much convincing for him to accept the Light. I learned to often bite my lip to try to keep a straight face, after one of the spirits angrily accused me of laughing at him! I feel much compassion and love for them, but I also understand that their suffering will soon be over; the length of time it takes them to accept the Light!

Pierre

— It is certain that you don't have the same perspective as an ordinary person who sees death as the *end* of something; that they are deprived of their life.

Carole

— One thing I do know is that if I let my emotions enter every time, I wouldn't be able to function very long. Some cases touch me more than others. On several different occasions, we had cases of little girls who had been murdered, who were brought to us by a Spirit Nun. A few of them had their bodies dismembered! Some of them asked me why that man had done that to them. I would explain that he was very sick in his mind, and I would put my arms around them and gently talk them into the Light. The thought of the inhumanity of sick minds that could do such things to innocent little children shook me to the very core of my being. Even though I tried to keep things in perspective in my own mind, realizing that there must have been "karma" working out in some area of their lives, on those nights I usually didn't sleep too well!

Pierre

— So we have no idea what we are going to see, or what is going to happen here tonight?

Carole

— No, because it's a new experience for us! When we do this work at my center, the lights are very low, and we only have a candle sitting on a stool in the center of the circle of people who are participating. Since I have known that we would be doing the program, where we would be working with spot lights on Rose, we have been practicing by putting the lights a little stronger each time to see if it would work just as well. The vibrations in this place are very different from the ones in my spiritual center.

Pierre
 — So we won't be able to watch her go into her trance state because of this fact?

Carole
 — It might possibly take too long because of the difference in energy. Usually it only takes me about thirty seconds to put her in a state of trance; but tonight I may have to put her through a period of relaxation to do so, and it might take as long as ten minutes.

We prepared to bring Rose to her place, and set an extra chair for Philippe, who would be serving as a "battery" for the extra energy we might need. He was a young man in his late twenties and had been a part of my center for awhile, taking development classes with me. Later on he also became the center's vice-president. Our energies were very compatible because he had the same astrological sign and ascendant as I did, Aries with a Sagittarius ascendant. A medium with whom he had a reading told him: "The person who is your teacher in this lifetime, has taught you in many others"; and when I had a reading with a deep trance medium who worked with a group of guides who would answer our questions on any subject, I just gave his name and asked if we had been together before. They said we had several lifetimes where we had worked together in healing, one of them was in Atlantis and another was a Kahuna lifetime, in the area where the Hawaiian Islands are today. They said that in both of those lifetimes, we had been brothers, me being the older; and I had taught him healing. I wasn't surprised, for when he walked into the center and we would hug as we greeted each other, I would often say: "Hello, little brother!"

Rose was smiling and well prepared mentally. She sat in her chair, very relaxed. She had been working with me for about three years, and besides her trance work, she was the secretary of our center. She transcribed and typed the seance tapes, and helped organize all the activities which were going on at different times. We were very close friends and had a lot of confidence in each other; so it was very easy for me to serve as her control for her trance state. We used to laugh at the way she would go under so fast! I always teach my students to start their relaxation by the feet and work up. I would say: "your toes are relaxing... your feet... your calves... your knees are relaxing... but the moment I said "knees", this was her catalyst to go out like a light! Her head would fall to her chest immediately, and would stay that way until the first spirit took over her body and lifted her head back up. Then I knew it was time to get to work! Rose was a real pro and this time was no different; a few minutes and she was gone!

The Rescue Cases Done On T.V.

The first case was a young man. As he came in, he was very frightened! He jerked himself back in his chair, and threw his arms up over his face.

Carole

— Good evening, friend, what is happening? No, It's alright... It's alright! My name is Carole; can you tell me your name? You don't need to be afraid, everything is fine. Why are you afraid?

Spirit
  – DON'T COME AND GET ME!

Carole
  – Where are you?

Spirit
  – I'M STUCK IN THAT THING BUT I DON'T WANT TO COME OUT!

Carole
  – You don't want to come out?

Spirit
  – No, I'M SCARED! THEY'LL FIND ME AND THEY'LL KILL ME! THEY'LL KILL ME... I'M AFRAID, LEAVE ME HERE!

Carole
  – It's alright love, I'll help you to come out.

Spirit
  – I'M TOO SCARED, THEY'LL KILL ME!

Carole
  – No, they won't, I'm going to help you! Do you see the white Light in front of you?

Spirit
  – WHAT IS THAT WHITE LIGHT?

Carole
  – It is to get you out, and to help you. After that, you will be alright. No one will hurt you, I will protect you. Can you tell me your name?

Spirit
  – IT IS FABIEN!

Carole
  – What happened, Fabien?

Spirit

– THEY SAID THAT I SOLD THEM OUT; BUT IT WASN'T ME, AND NOW THEY WANT TO KILL ME! THEY SAY THAT I'M A STOOL PIGEON AND IT'S NOT TRUE; I'M NOT A STOOL... IT'S NOT TRUE!

Carole

– It's alright, I'm going to help you.

Spirit

– ARE YOU SURE? BECAUSE I HAVE TO HAVE CONFIDENCE IN YOU. I'M SCARED! I'M ALRIGHT HERE IN THIS HOLE.

Carole

– It's going to be O.K. I am going to take you to some people who will help you. Do you see the Light?

Spirit

– (Very Frightened) YES.

Carole

– You're going to climb into this Light.

Spirit

– ALONE? (He jerks back and shakes his head).

Carole

– Yes, but there are some friends of mine who will help you; this is like an elevator, Fabien. And when you get to the top, my friends are going to help you, and no one will ever hurt you again! (He was very hesitant.) Trust me Fabien.

Spirit

– YOU'RE SURE THERE IS NO ONE AROUND?

Carole

– No, it's alright, there is no one who will hurt you; I've sent them all away. Do you see the elevator? Just get in.

Spirit

– I'M GOING TO RUN... I'M IN IT NOW!

Carole

– Push the button. Do you feel it moving up?

Spirit

– YES.

Carole

– When you get to the top and feel it stopping, let me know. Has it stopped now?

Spirit

– YES.

Carole

– Now the door will open.

Spirit

– THEY'RE NOT COMING TO GET ME, ARE THEY?

Carole

– No, those are friends of mine. Can you see them now?

Spirit

– YES, THEY HAVE KIND FACES.

Carole

– These are friends of mine and they won't hurt you. Go with them and they will explain everything to you.

Spirit

– ARE THEY GOING TO TREAT ME, MY BACK AND EVERYWHERE ELSE THAT HURTS?

Carole

– What happened? They gave you a good beating, didn't they?

Spirit

– THEY CHASED ME FOR A LONG TIME. I FINALLY FOUND A PLACE TO HIDE FROM THEM... LOOK AT MY BACK.

Carole
- The Doctors are going to take care of you and I will come
and see you later.

Spirit
- YOU TOLD ME YOUR NAME IS CAROLE? I THANK YOU
VERY MUCH, LADY; AND IF I COME OUT OF THE
HOSPITAL, YOU'LL COME AND SEE ME?

Carole
- Yes, or you come and see me.

Spirit
- I WOULD LIKE THAT, AND IF I EVER HAVE TO GO
TO COURT, YOU'LL COME WITH ME, O.K.?

Carole
- O.K. and I give you a big hug.

Spirit
- AND I RETURN YOUR HUG. GOOD-BYE.

Case # 2

Rose's face and body movements changed into those of
a small child, with a little grin on her face that made her
big dimples stand out. The voice changed completely, and
it was like that of a small little child with a lisp.

Carole
- Hello!
Spirit
- HI!
Carole
- What is your name?
Spirit
- CECILE. (The lisp made it hard to understand.)

Carole
  − Gisele?

Spirit
  − No! CECILE!

Carole
  − Oh, It's Cecile! I'm sorry, I didn't understand! How old are you?

Spirit
  − (Holds up four fingers) FOUR YEARS OLD!

Carole
  − You're four years old!

Spirit
  − (Nods Her Head)... I'M GOING TO SCHOOL SOON, TO KINDERGARTEN.

Carole
  − What are you doing?

Spirit
  − I WAS PLAYING WITH SOME LITTLE GIRLS; AND THEY ALL LEFT! (She is playing with her hands and grinning.)

Carole
  − They all left!

Spirit
  − YES, ALL OF THEM, AND I'M ALL ALONE. (Says with sad voice.)

Carole
  − You're all alone...

Spirit
  − WHY DID THEY GO?

Carole
  − I don't know why. Where are you?

Spirit
- CAN'T YOU SEE I'M IN A HOSPITAL BED?

Carole
- Oh, you're in a hospital bed!

Spirit
- YES, AND THEY WANT ME TO GO; AND I DON'T WANT TO GO!

Carole
- Where do they want you to go?

Spirit
- OVER THERE!

Carole
- And you don't want to go!

Spirit
- NO! GO AND GET MOMMY!

Carole
- What is your mommy's name?

Spirit
- (Shocked that I didn't know.) WELL, IT'S MOMMY!

Carole
- You don't know her other name?

Spirit
- IT'S MOMMY! DO YOU KNOW MY MOMMY'S OTHER NAME?

Carole
- No, I don't know your mommy's name either.

Spirit
- WELL, IT'S MOMMY!

Carole
- O.K., it's mommy! We'll go and get your mommy! We'll both go and get her, would you like that?

Spirit

— YES! (Flashes me a grin from ear to ear.)

Carole

— Do you see the Light in front of you?

Spirit

— YES, BUT I WANT TO TAKE MY DOLL.

Carole

— Yes, bring your doll sweetheart. What is your doll's name?

Spirit

— CHOU CHOU!

Carole

— Chou! Chou! Oh she's beautiful, isn't she?

Spirit

— YES!

Carole

— O.K. We're going to take Chou Chou, and go and find mommy! Do you see the pretty Light in front of you?

Spirit

— YES, BUT BEFORE I GO I HAVE SOMETHING TO ASK YOU. YOU'RE NOT AN AUNTIE, ARE YOU?

Carole

— No, I'm not an Auntie, I'm a friend.

Spirit

— CAUSE ALL THE AUNTIES... ALL IN WHITE!

Carole

— Oh, all the Aunties are dressed in white. What color is my dress?

Spirit

— BLUE! (My blouse was fuschia.)

Carole

– Oh, it's a pretty blue, isn't it? Look at the lovely Light. We're going to find mommy.

Spirit

– ARE YOU GOING TO BUY ME SOME CRAYONS SO I CAN COLOR?

Carole

– Yes, and I'll buy you a coloring book too. Have you climbed into the Light?

Spirit

– YES.

Carole

– You'll be able to talk to me, but I won't go and see you until later.

Spirit

– OH... CECILE IS SCARED ALONE...

Carole

– You're scared alone? No, you don't have to be afraid, I'll be there very soon.

Spirit

– YES? O.K. BUT HURRY.

Carole

– The door just closed and you are going up.

Spirit

– HEY... IT WENT ZOOM... NOW IT'S STOPPED.

Carole

– The door is opening. Who is there?

Spirit

– HEY, IT'S GRANDPA! GRANDPA, WHAT ARE YOU DOING HERE? YOU'VE COME TO GET ME? YOU'VE COME TO GET CECILE! YES? (We could see that she was listening to someone who was talking to her)... HE SAYS THAT MOMMY IS VERY SICK...

Carole

– Oh, you're mommy is sick, and Grandpa is going to take care of you.

Spirit

– BUT GRANDPA HAS GONE FOR A LONG SLEEP! MOMMY SAID: "GRANDPA IS GOING TO SLEEP FOR A LONG, LONG TIME!"

Carole

– Well, go with Grandpa.

Spirit

– HEY, HE WOKE UP!

Carole

– Yeah, he woke up; go with Grandpa.

Spirit

– O.K., I'LL GO WITH GRANDPA! (She was all excited.) GOOD-BYE!

Carole

– Good-bye Sweetheart. (She threw me a big noisy kiss with her hand as she left.)

Case # 3

He came in and was holding his hands crossed about six inches from his chest. I could see that the hands were crippled. He was very wary, and didn't seem too happy at being there. He pronounced each word distinctly, as if he were angry.

Carole

– Good evening. What's happening?

Spirit

– WHY DID YOU BRING ME HERE?

Carole

- You came to see me, don't you remember? It's because you need help. Don't you know what happened?

Spirit

- WHERE ARE WE?

Carole

- What do you remember about where you were?

Spirit

- I WAS SITTING AT HOME!

Carole

- You were sitting at home, and what happened? Were you sick?

Spirit

- WELL, DOESN'T IT SHOW? CRIPPLED LIKE I AM!

Carole

- You're crippled!

Spirit

- YEAH!

Carole

- You don't remember what happened?

Spirit

- FROM WHAT I REMEMBER, IT SEEMS LIKE TWO MEN CAME IN AND THEY WANTED TO HURT ME! THAT'S ALL! (He was beginning to trust me and his voice softened.)

Carole

- You don't remember anything else?

Spirit

- NO, MY HEAD HURTS!

Carole

- I think they hurt you, didn't they?

Spirit

 — YEAH!

Carole

 — Well, I'm going to send you to a place where they will give you medical treatment. Can you tell me your name?

Spirit

 — YES, GABRIEL!

Carole

 — Where do you live, Gabriel?

Spirit

 — (Suddenly became very cautious) WHO DO YOU WORK FOR. DO YOU WORK FOR THE POLICE?

Carole

 — No, I don't work for the police.

Spirit

 — (Lowers Voice) BECAUSE YOU'RE NOT THE WOMAN FROM WELFARE.

Carole

 — No, I'm not from welfare; I am only someone who came to help you because you needed help. How old are you?

Spirit

 — SIXTEEN.

Carole

 — You're only sixteen. My goodness, you're not very old, are you?

Spirit

 — No!

Carole

 — I'm going to help you, Gabriel. Do you see that big Light right in front of you? It's like an elevator. You're going to advance and get in, and it will take you up.

Spirit
– (Shakes His Head) I CAN'T MOVE TO GET INTO IT.

Carole
– O.K., we'll bring a stretcher to you. Do you see it in front of you?

Spirit
– YES! HELP ME!

Carole
– Yes, we'll put you on! Now you're on, and moving towards the Light. O.K.? Now it's going to move up, and there will be doctors waiting for you when you reach the top. They'll take X-rays and see what your problems are. I think you got a bad beating, didn't you?

Spirit
– I KNOW I HURT ALL OVER!

Carole
– Is it going up?

Spirit
– YES.

Carole
– I want you to tell me when it stops.

Spirit
– IT HAS STOPPED.

Carole
– The door will open and a doctor will come and get you. (He starts to sob and can't speak.) It's O.K. Love, who is there?

Spirit
– (Still Crying) IT'S MOMMA!

Carole
– Your momma is there?

Spirit

– BUT MOMMA IS DEAD. I'M NOT DEAD, AM I, LADY?

Carole

– Go with your mother and she will explain everything to you.

Spirit

– YES. BUT WHY DID THEY DO THAT TO ME?

Carole

– I don't know, sweetheart!

Spirit

– COME TO ME, MOMMA. HELP ME! (Still Sobbing.)

Carole

– Go with your mother, Gabriel; she has come to get you. You have finished suffering. I'll go and see you.

Case # 4

He came in with his right hand up to his throat and was coughing, complaining that he was choking. It is difficult sometimes to know exactly what is happening, because I stay very grounded to do this work. I am not in an altered state of consciousness, and sometimes I have to ask more questions than others.

Spirit

– I'M CHOKING! I'M CHOKING!

Carole

– It's alright! (I make the movement with my right hand of taking something away from his throat, because I'm still not sure what is happening.) Do you have a pain in your chest?

Spirit

– NO! CAN'T YOU SEE? (He seems to be trying to loosen

something around his neck, and is speaking in a way that sounds as if he is strangling.)

Carole
— Do you have a rope around your neck? (I pretend that I am removing it.) It's alright now, it's gone. You can breathe now! Take a big breath and you will see that you can breathe now.

Spirit
— BUT IT FEELS AS IF IT'S ALL SWOLLEN INSIDE!

Carole
— Look, I'm taking away all the pain. Now you can breathe better. What happened to you?

Spirit
— MY GOD! I WAS DISCOURAGED!

Carole
— You were discouraged! How old are you?

Spirit
— TWENTY-ONE.

Carole
— My Goodness! It's not funny to be discouraged at 21 years old, is it?

Spirit
— OH, BUT LIFE IS SO HARD! (It was so sad to hear him speak in a low voice with so much discouragement.) MAYBE YOU SAVED ME ONCE AGAIN!

Carole
— Have you tried this before? It's not the first time?

Spirit
— (Shakes his head) LOOK AT MY WRISTS. IT'S LIKE THERE IS ALWAYS SOMEONE AT THE LAST MINUTE TO SAVE MY LIFE.

Carole

– What is your name?

Spirit

– EMILE.

Carole

– I am going to help you, Emile. We are going to take you to the hospital, alright?

Spirit

– IT'S BECAUSE I'M NOT SUPPOSED TO DIE!

Carole

– No, you're not allowed to take your life! God gave you a life; He didn't give it to you for you to take it away. You have something to live for here on Earth!

Spirit

– YES, BUT NOT THE WAY WE LIVE!

Carole

– It's not easy, is it? Look In front of you, Emile. Do you see the lovely white Light?

Spirit

– YES.

Carole

– O.K., We are going to advance into that Light; it's like an elevator. This will take you to the hospital! Are you in now? It will go up. You tell me when it stops.

Spirit

– IT IS STOPPING.

Carole

– The door will open.

Spirit

– THERE IS A LIGHT THAT IS VERY BRIGHT! (He puts his arm up over his face to shade his eyes.)

Carole
> – That's good. Do you see any people around?

Spirit
> – I SEE ONLY THE LOWER LEGS! HEY! THEY DON'T HAVE ANY SHOES ON!

Carole
> – This is a special hospital. Is there someone there? Can you see any faces?

Spirit
> – I'M TRYING TO SEE; THERE ARE SO MANY OF THEM! THEY'RE ALL HOLDING THEIR ARMS OUT TO ME! I'VE NEVER FELT SO MUCH LOVE IN MY WHOLE LIFE!

Carole
> – You need love, Sweetheart, that's why they're all holding their arms out to you.

Spirit
> – ARE ALL THE NURSES LIKE THAT?

Carole
> – Of course.

Spirit
> – IF I HAD BEEN LOVED LIKE THAT ON EARTH... HEY I JUST THOUGHT OF SOMETHING, I KNOW I'M NOT NORMAL, BECAUSE I SEE THEM, AND I TRY TO TOUCH THEM, AND MY HAND GOES RIGHT THROUGH...

Carole
> – What do you think that means?

Spirit
> – I GUESS I SUCCEEDED THIS TIME!

Carole
> – Go with them, my love, they'll explain everything to you.

Spirit

— WELL... I GUESS I REALLY DID IT THIS TIME!

Carole

— Go with them and they'll help you.

Spirit

— BUT IF I DIDN'T MISS THIS TIME, HOW COME I CAN TALK TO YOU AND YOU ANSWER ME... IF I'M DEAD, I'M DEAD?

Carole

— Yes, But I can talk to you just the same, because I can help you.

Spirit

— YES? WELL I'LL LEAVE NOW.

Carole

— Go with them Sweetheart, you will be happy there.

Spirit

— ANYWAY, IF I COULD HAVE KNOWN LOVE ON EARTH LIKE WHAT I FEEL FROM THESE PEOPLE WHO ARE HOLDING THEIR ARMS OUT TO ME, I DON'T THINK I WOULD EVER HAVE DONE IT!

Carole

— I understand.

Spirit

— I THANK YOU FOR BRINGING ME THERE.

Carole

— I was happy to help you Emile; God Bless you.

Spirit

— I'M NOT ANXIOUS TO PASS TO THE OTHER SIDE! ANYWAY, THERE'S NOTHING I CAN DO ABOUT IT... WHAT'S DONE IS DONE!

Carole
- You'll have another chance! God is a just God, but you have to forgive yourself.

Spirit
- YES, BUT IF I HAVE TO COME BACK TO EARTH AGAIN, HOW WILL I DO IT?

Carole
- You'll be ready the next time; they will explain everything to you over there. You're going to rest for a while first.

Spirit
- WELL, ANYWAY... GOOD-BYE.

Case # 5

This was the hardest case for me emotionally, although I didn't let it show! It was a little girl who was raped and murdered; and you will see as she comes in, how everything was erased from the conscious mind until I triggered it, to get her to accept the Light.

Carole
- Hello.

Spirit
- HELLO!

Carole
- What's your name?

Spirit
- JOSEE.

Carole
- How old are you Josee?

Spirit
- I'M EIGHT YEARS OLD.

Carole
- What are you doing?

Spirit
- I'M GOING TO A BIRTHDAY PARTY.

Carole
- Is it the birthday of a little friend?

Spirit
- YES, IT'S CARMEN'S BIRTHDAY.

Carole
- Did you buy her a gift?

Spirit
- OF COURSE, I'M TYING THE BOW. (She had her hands in her lap and was moving her fingers continually when she came in. Now I knew the reason for this.)

Carole
- What did you buy her?

Spirit
- I BOUGHT HER A LITTLE MIRROR TO PUT ON HER BUREAU.

Carole
- Good; she'll be happy, won't she?

Spirit
- I HOPE SO.

Carole
- (She hadn't given me enough details for me to understand her situation, or how she had passed.) Where do you live?

Spirit
- I LIVE HERE! (I knew that whatever it was, it must have happened at home.)

Carole
- Are you alone in the house?

Spirit
- YES.

Carole
- Mommy and daddy are gone?

Spirit
- YES, THEY HAVE GONE TO THE MOVIES.

Carole
- They've gone to the movies and you're alone in the house!

Spirit
- YES!

Carole
- You've finished tying your bow, and now what is happening?

Spirit
- (By trying to remember, she triggers the memory. It takes a few moments, then she pulls back in her chair and starts to panic. Her eyes widen, and her face becomes terror stricken, and she starts to sob. She wraps her arms around her body and gently starts to rock.) LADY! SAVE ME! SAVE ME FROM THAT MAN! SAVE ME! NO! NO! MISTER... DON'T TOUCH ME. NO... NO... (Through all of this I am trying to convince her that I am helping her, and am sending him away! By using my energy and making movements with my hand around her head, I am completely eliminating the picture from her mind.)

Carole
- He's gone, sweetheart. See? He's not there anymore. Are you alright?

Spirit

— HE TORE MY DRESS!

Carole

— He's gone now! We're going to change your dress and you can go on to your party, O.K.? He wasn't nice, was he?

Spirit

— (Her chest still heaving from the huge sobs.) No!

Carole

— You're going to come with me now, alright?

Spirit

— YES!

Carole

— Do you see the pretty white Light in front of you?

Spirit

— YES!

Carole

— You're going to get into that Light; it's like an elevator, and it's going to take you somewhere.

Spirit

— BUT I'M AFRAID.

Carole

— No, you don't have to be afraid, some friends of mine are going to meet you. Will you give me your gift? (She hands it to me.) We'll put it aside, and when you come back, you can go to Carmen's party. We just want to be sure you're alright.

Spirit

— MY DRESS IS ALL TORN AND I'M SAD. (She was still trying to work out the emotions of the experience.)

Carole

— It's all over sweetheart, don't worry about it any more.

We're going to get you another pretty dress! What color would you like?

Spirit

— BLUE.

Carole

— O.K., we'll find you a pretty blue dress. You are going to come into the Light now, and we will have a nice blue dress waiting for you up there. Don't cry anymore love, it's all over.

Spirit

— (Still hiccuping from the crying.) YOU WON'T TELL MOMMY WHAT HAPPENED?

Carole

— No, we won't tell your mommy, O.K.? Are you in the Light now? We're going to go and get you a pretty blue dress.

Spirit

— YES.

Carole

— The door will open and you will see some friends of mine who are coming to get you, Josee, alright? They will have a nice blue dress for you.

Spirit

— IT HAS STOPPED.

Carole

— The door will open.

Spirit

— WHY ARE THEY ALL DRESSED IN LONG GOWNS?

Carole

— Because that's the way they dress there.

Spirit

— BUT I WON'T HAVE A LONG DRESS!

Carole

– We'll find you a lovely long blue dress. Would you like that?

Spirit

– YES, THAT WOULD BE VERY NICE OF YOU.

Carole

– Do you see any people that you know?

Spirit

– NO, BUT THERE IS A LADY WITH SOME FLOWERS.

Carole

– Oh! Isn't that nice of her! I think she wants you to take them to Carmen's party.

Spirit

– THAT'S POSSIBLE.

Carole

– She wants you to go with her. Go with her, honey!

Spirit

– YES, BUT I WANT TO GO TO CARMEN'S PARTY!

Carole

– She'll find you a blue dress, and then you can go.

Spirit

– THAT IS FINE. PLEASE DON'T TELL MOMMY WHAT HAPPENED, ALRIGHT?

Carole

– We won't tell her.

Spirit

– ALRIGHT! GOOD-BYE AND THANK YOU.

We really have to watch the video to fully appreciate the above cases! Because Rose is in a deep trance state, the look on her face, the emotions, the changes in the voice, are exactly those of the spirit coming through. I often wondered what the viewers felt while watching the last case. To this day, I still have trouble watching it! But I wondered how many men out there who have molested little children, might have watched it, and felt a sense of guilt! I have no idea if the murderer of Josee was caught; because my work is not to help them find justice for what happened in this lifetime, but to let their spirit find peace, by going to the Light. I know that one of the little girls who was murdered, and who was brought to us by a Nun, came back shortly after and gave us many details of her death. She said that the Nun had told them not to give us their real names when we did the rescue, because we would want to investigate, and it was no longer of any importance.

Chapter Ten

LIFE AND DEATH OF STEPHANE

Stephane was born on the 10th of September 1970, the first of a family of two children. His brother was born seven years later. He lived all of his life in the same small town where his mother was raised, issue of a very large French Canadian family. During many of those years, his dad worked for an international company on huge projects hundreds of miles away, coming home for periods of rest when he could.

As Stephane grew older and into his difficult teen years, he went through periods of feeling misunderstood. He always felt different from other boys. No matter how hard he tried, whatever he did, nothing turned out the way he wanted. Between two brothers with completely different personalities, sibling rivalry is always very strong; so it was with them. He had a need to help other people, whether it was family members or friends, and always refused to take money for what he did. Other kids his age considered this dumb and often called him stupid! Always the first to offer his services for volunteer work, people knew they could depend on him. This may have been Stephane's way of buying the love and appreciation he needed so badly for his own self esteem, and he felt frustrated and put down by the mean things that were often said to him.

In April 1991, Stephane started complaining of pains in his abdomen. His mother took him to the doctor, who diagnosed a polyp on his intestine, and sent him to the hospital for treatment. It was decided that an operation was needed. Complications developed that necessitated four months of care in two different hospitals. He suffered a great deal from all of the treatments and was very lonely.

He was a different person when he came out of the hospital in the middle of August. Things started to change in his life and he was the happiest he had ever been. Everything in his life that hadn't worked before, and caused him so much unhappiness, just seemed to fall into place. He kept telling his mother how happy he was and marveled that he could feel this way! He would say, "Mom, I'm not sick anymore! Mom, I'm so happy with my new car!" (His parents bought it for him as a birthday present.) He also met a young girl and they were happy together. It looked as if it would continue. Stephane was a drummer with a band and they started getting more contracts, which was another source of his joy. He was becoming so good that people told him he was a real "pro". He said to his mother, "Mom, I have to tell you frankly, I don't know what is happening! I am so happy. It is like all of a sudden everything is falling into my lap from Heaven!" This made his mother very happy because several times in the past, when things were going badly, he would stand with his hand held out and say: "Jesus, why don't you come and get me? What am I doing on this earth? I've had two accidents and you've helped me avoid other ones. You should have come and gotten me, Jesus. I would be so happy with you!" His mother would answer, "My God, what are you saying? I only have two children and I love you both. You break my heart when you say these things!"

One of Stephane's aunts, whose husband was working out of the Province, had a heart problem and was unable to stay alone. She asked him if he would move in so she would have someone in the house with her. Being the helpful person he was, Stephane accepted. On the 23rd of September 1991, he was on his way to take some personal belongings to his aunt's place, and decided to stop and show his new car to an uncle. A young man from another town was there, and needed a ride to a nearby city. Since Stephane would be going there after dropping his clothes off at his aunt's house, he agreed to take him. Because the boy was in a hurry, he agreed to leave at once. As they came off the country road to get onto the highway he made his stop. They looked both ways, but the leaves on a tree blocked their view. He advanced a little and stopped again. They both looked again and he moved onto the highway but a car coming to his left struck him broadside!

It was 5:55 p.m. Because the vehicle was so badly damaged, it took an hour to get Stephane out of the car and into the ambulance. His father was notified at 7:00 p.m. and went immediately to the hospital. They told him they would have to operate, but he was just too badly injured. On September 24th, at 1:05 a.m. Stephane passed to the World of Spirit without regaining consciousness!

His mother, Gaetane, didn't want to go to the hospital and see him in the state in which she knew he would be, so she decided to stay at home with her younger son to pray. His father, Guy, came home at 1:45 a.m. As he came in the door she asked him what was happening. He didn't respond and his face was gray; Gaetane knew the answer! She said that in her heart she accepted the accident. "The Lord gave Stephane to me for 21 years, and now He has come and taken him back!" It wasn't easy to accept, but there was nothing else she could do. Her husband was taking Stephane's death so badly that she knew she had to be the strong one in the family to get them through this ordeal.

Beginning Of The Manifestations

When Stephane's father arrived home and walked in the door, the cat came up to him and let out a very loud "meow", then he ran into the living room to hide. His wife felt that the cat understood what had happened, as pets are very psychic. In the following days the cat seemed to sense Stephane's presence in different parts of the house, in the corner, and at the foot of the stairs. His ears would perk up and the hair on his back would stand up as he stood there staring at those spots. Sometimes he would go up and lie on Stephane's bed, as if he knew that he was there in the room with him. The cat's behavior pattern had completely changed.

Eugene and Colette, friends from the band, came to the house often. Eugene especially was very psychic. They had both participated in seances at different times, through the use of the ouija board and automatic writing. They came to help the family; and it also helped them in their own grief, as they both loved him very much, and Stephane always called Colette "my little sister", the one he never had. Whenever they went, Eugene sensed Stephane's presence strongly and the room would become very cold. The whole family had shivers going up and down their bodies and often felt a cool breeze. But when you have had no experience with this phenomena, you don't know what is occurring; you think, perhaps the house has cooled off and the heat needs to be turned up. It's only when you look back and remember the strange happenings that you realize that it was not normal!

Stephane kept his drums in a spare room upstairs, near his own room, where he often practiced. One day after his passing, his brother was sitting at the drums, and he put a tape in the tape recorder, as he had often seen Stephane do. He started playing the drums to the beat of the music. When the song was finished, he had the sticks in his hand and turned to change the tape; but, as he did so, the beat of the drums continued with no one touching them. This really frightened him. He jumped up, threw down the drum sticks, and ran down the stairs to tell his mother and father what had transpired! He was as white as a sheet and in a state of shock. On another occasion they had company, and were all downstairs when they heard the drums start to play for about a minute. They knew that there was no one upstairs. Another time, with the family all downstairs, the music suddenly started up in the ceiling for a few moments.

Manifestations With Relatives And Friends

Most of the members of Gaetane's large family lived within a few miles of each other, and they started having phenomena occur in their homes. It were as if Stephane, unable to draw attention to his astral presence in his own home, was trying every way he could to get his message across.

Sister # 1

One night she and her husband were sleeping in their bedroom. The youngest daughter was sleeping in her room in the basement, and an older daughter was out to a party. Around 1:00 a.m. she was awakened by the sound of the T.V. being turned on in the living room. She surmised that her daughter had arrived and turned it on; but, on verifying, found that she had not yet come home. She turned the T.V. off and went back to bed; but, a short while later, the T.V. was on again. The daughter had not yet arrived home. This happened again at 3:45 a.m. and she turned the set off once more. Although this had never happened before, it never entered her mind that it could be a manifestation from Stephane, because these things were unknown to her. The next morning she talked to her daughter about it. She replied, "Mom, Stephane came to visit you. Who else do you think would turn the T.V. on?" In manifestations from the World of Spirit, things often seem to happen three times, as with "spirit raps"; it is always *three* sharp raps on the wall or on the door. She shared this experience with other members of the family, and they started admitting that they also were having things happen that they were unable to explain!

Sister # 2

One night, the aunt with whom Stephane was supposed to live for awhile, was having her supper in her kitchen in the basement when she heard footsteps up over her head, as if someone were walking around. Her neighbor had been piling wood in his yard, and she thought it must be him going back to finish, after having his own supper. She didn't think anymore about it. The next night, the neighbor was no longer working in his yard; but the sound of the same heavy footsteps started up again. She realized that it was possibly her nephew who was walking around upstairs. She went to the foot of the stairs and said, "Stephane, I know you liked to come and eat with me and I'd love to have you join me, but it's impossible. So please go back to where you came from." He came on three occasions close together and each time she would talk to him gently and lovingly, and he would leave.

Sister # 3

She was in her house and suddenly heard the outside door open. She thought it was one of her children coming in; but after a few minutes, when no one came into the room, she went to look. There was no one there, so she closed the door. It immediately opened again and she closed it once more. When it happened a third time, she thought one of the kids was playing a trick on her. She stepped outside to look around, but there was no one near the house. Suddenly she heard three sharp raps coming from under the balcony! It gave her a shock and really scared her, but she felt that possibly it was Stephane, trying to make his presence known. He would also come in the night and tap her on the shoulder when she was in bed. Sometimes it happened several times in the same night, until she was having difficulty getting any sleep. Finally she got angry and told him, "Stephane, that's enough! I don't want to see you in my house anymore!", and it was finished; he never manifested there again.

Sister # 4

She would feel something beside her bed. The room would get so cold that she would lay there shivering, with the blankets pulled up to her nose. Finally she said to him, "Don't scare me, Stephane. You know I always liked you! I have to get some sleep, so please don't scare me!" Immediately she would feel the cold dissipating, and the room start to warm up.

Brother

He is my son Mike's friend, and, although he sometimes pretends to be tough, Mike says he is one of the most sensitive people he knows. However, I don't think he has much knowledge of what happens in the afterlife. He was having a problem with the well, and went to the basement to check the pump. He went down the steps and walked past his heavy one piece jumpsuit that was hanging on the wall. It was the kind of suit Canadians wear when they ride their snowmobiles. As he walked past it, one of the sleeves lifted up by itself and gave him three sharp taps on his shoulder! He was so shocked that he didn't know what to say or do. The pump was on the floor in the corner, and as he bent down to examine it, he suddenly sensed a very strong presence right behind him; he said it felt as if a wall were building up. He jumped up, swung around, and said, "Stephane, I know you are here!", and headed up the stairs as fast as he could. Something like this is a real shock to a nonbeliever!

Eugene & Colette

The band in which Stephane played belonged to Eugene and his partner in life, Colette, and the three had been very good friends. They appreciated Stephane's good qualities as well as his musical talent. The evening of the day of the accident, something kept pushing Eugene to go to the hospital to see Colette who was working the 3 to 11 shift as a secretary in the radiology department. When he arrived, she told him that Stephane had been in a very bad accident and was at the hospital in a critical condition. As soon as her shift was finished, they both went up to the third floor to join Stephane's dad, who was waiting for news from the operating room. They stayed with him until 11:30, when they had to leave to pick up their children. At approximately 1:00 a.m., Eugene awoke with a start. He awakened Colette to tell her to "listen to the music", but she couldn't hear anything. The next morning she called Stephane's mother and was told that he had died around 1:00 a.m. But it was as if Eugene already knew it; because Stephane had come to tell him, at the exact moment he had passed, by somehow playing music that only he with his psychic and spiritual gifts, could hear.

One night after the funeral, they were visiting Stephane's parents. While sitting downstairs in the kitchen, the clock suddenly started to tick very fast and became much louder than usual. Eugene sensed Stephane's presence, and he indicated to Eugene that he wanted to speak to his mother. However, Eugene told him she was too nervous because of all his manifestations in the house. A few times when they were there, they would hear music start up in the ceiling and two beats on the drum at 1:00 a.m. They could always sense his presence and the house would get very cold. One night at work, while Colette was typing a text concerning Stephane, the typewriter suddenly started typing by itself and really frightened her. She told him, "If it's you, Stephane, please stop, because you're scaring me". Immediately all was quiet. The night prior to the day that I had arranged to do the soul rescue work in the family home, he kept Eugene awake most of the night. He was manifesting his joy and excitement at the prospect of being able to talk to his mother the next day. Eugene, being so open to that side of life and because of the "love link" he had with Stephane, was unable to get any sleep.

Approximately three weeks later, Guy left Gaetane alone in the house for the first time since the accident. He had taken their other son to a hockey game in which the young boy was playing. Gaetane wasn't afraid, but when she went up to Stephane's room she could sense his presence. As she walked in different parts of the house, Gaetane would feel shivers all over her body. A cousin called to see how she was, and she was very happy to have someone to talk to so that the time would pass faster. Gaetane started hearing a strange sound in the house and asked her cousin to hold the line while she checked it out. As she took the receiver away from her ear, she heard what sounded like someone snoring very loudly. There was crying and sobbing coming from Stephane's room upstairs! As she turned back to the phone, Gaetane said there was something very strange happening in the house; she was sure it was Stephane, but she didn't know what to do about it. The cousin answered that it was impossible, because Stephane was dead. This was a person who had no knowledge of, or belief in, the afterlife. But the phenomena only got louder and Gaetane's ears started to ring. She was freezing and the hair started to stand up all over her body. Scared to death, she felt glued to her chair and very weak. It stopped as quickly as it had started, and Gaetane continued her conversation, although she still felt the weakness in her arms and legs. A few minutes later it started up again even louder than the first time, and it sounded as if his bed was rocking from the vibrations of the loud sobbing and lamentations coming from Stephane's bedroom. Gaetane's cousin told her to run out of the house and go to a neighbor's; but it was raining hard outside, and she felt so weak. Gaetane knew that if she tried to get up off her chair she would fall to the floor! Then the music started coming from the ceiling. It was not music that she could identify, but was definitely coming from upstairs and through the ceiling. Gaetane was so frightened that she wouldn't let her cousin hang up the phone until Guy arrived home.

The next day was Friday, the day for Gaetane's weekly appointment with her hairdresser, Michelyne, who was one of my best friends and confidante. Each week, she shared the manifestations happening to the different members of the family with her. When Michelyne asked her if they were still having problems, Gaetane told her what had transpired the night before in her own home. She couldn't take any more! What she didn't know was that Michelyne, knowing about my work in soul rescue and haunted houses, had mentioned these things to me and had asked if I wanted to do something about the phenomena. I had told her to tell Gaetane to get in touch with me if she wanted help. We had lived in the same town for twenty-five years, but she only knew me as a business woman, although I had been giving classes in my Spiritual center at the end of my home, and lecturing there for at least twelve of those years. I tried to follow the teachings of Christ as often as I could in my own life; and I always felt that He was right when He said, "You are never a prophet in your own country," which was the philosophy that He followed 2,000 years ago. I never mentioned my spiritual work to the local people, but my classes were always more than filled through word of mouth. People came to me for consultations from as far as 200 miles away. The local people who found their way to my door for help always said they found me "by coincidence," but all of us on the Spiritual path know, that an accident or a coincidence doesn't exist!

I had been lecturing and giving workshops in another province for five days. On arriving home on the Monday, her message was on my answering machine, so I called her that night, and briefly explained what happens when we pass to spirit, and what "soul rescue" was. Gaetane made an appointment for me to go to her house a few days later. She wanted to know who could be present at the seance. Of course this is something which intrigues everyone, even those who say they don't believe, and a few family members had asked if they could attend. I explained that this was not a *show* I was putting on for entertainment purposes. This task was very important and spiritual, and I wanted only the immediate family members to be present. She asked if her sister-in-law, who was very spiritual and had helped her so much through the ordeal, and the young couple in whose band Stephane played, who were interested in, and had some experience in Spiritualism, could be allowed to assist. I accepted.

The Seance

I arrived at Stephane's home at 10:00 a.m. Gaetane was waiting with her sister-in-law, Eugene and Colette, and Guy was expected at any moment. When he arrived, we all sat down and I spent half an hour explaining what happens when we die and what soul rescue is, and I coached them on the part they would play.

Knowing that the spirit who would be chanelling through was Stephane, I knew there was no danger involved for myself by doing it alone. However, it is more complicated, as I have to play a dual role. I am always conscious of what is happening, and if there is a complication, I tell them that it is me, (Carole) speaking, and explain the problem to them.

I felt Stephane's presence strongly on arriving, as the house had a certain chilly feeling that always tells me that spirit is present. He was very patient while I explained everything. However, as we lit the candles and incense, and moved into the living room to prepare for the seance, Stephane was becoming more excited and impatient. We sat with the chairs in a circle, and I told them what they could do to help; I asked them to sit with their hands in their laps, but focused towards me to help with the energy. I explained that, although one of my spiritual gifts was "Transfiguration", (My face transfigures completely into the face of the spirit coming through, and is easily recognizable), that was not the purpose of the seance. We needed to put Stephane into the Light as quickly and gently as possible, with acceptance on his part. I told them to speak very little and not ask for "earthly things such as the details of the accident, etc.," because he was already traumatized enough, and these things were no longer of any importance. We had hardly sat down, when already Stephane was trying to take over my body; he had been waiting long enough!

I sensed that Stephane was very close to his mother, and told Gaetane that she was to be the one to connect with him first. He had such powerful energy, because he had held his emotions back for so long, that when I finally permitted him to control, he came in sobbing very loudly and the tears poured down my face. Stephane started manifesting strongly, and cried, "Mom! Mom! Where am I? What's wrong? Why doesn't anyone answer me when I talk to them?" His mother came and stood in front of him, and started repeating over and over that he had to go to the Light. Stephane just sobbed louder and said, "What's happening? I speak to you, and you don't even answer me! I touch you, and my hand goes right through! What in hell is happening?" He was manifesting strongly in my body and the emotions were very high. That was when I realized that Stephane did not know that he had passed out of his body. I asked Gaetane to tell him about the accident, and that he had passed over. She immediately explained to him that he had been in an accident and had died, that now it was important for him to go to the Light he would see near him, as this would take him to God.

Because I was conscious of everything that was happening, I immediately sensed a change in his energy. As he listened to her, he finally understood why everyone around him seemed to be acting so strangely.

His mother moved closer and was standing just in front of him. Stephane reached out and put his arms around her, as she bent down to console him. He was crying very hard. Laying his head on her breast and sobbing, he released all the emotions which had built up over the past month when he must have felt so very rejected. He finally became calmer and more accepting of his situation, and was finally able to speak with less emotion. I could feel the love he had for his mother, as he hung on to her and absorbed the motherly love that was flowing to him. Gaetane said later, "Although it was Carole's body, there was no doubt whatsoever in my mind that it was my son, Stephane, that I held in my arms and consoled. When he laid his head on my shoulder, it was a man's head, and I rubbed his back and held his hand, and I know that it was Stephane's vibrations; and that I was holding my son's soul in my arms, even though he was in another physical body."

Stephane talked to his mother for a few minutes, telling her how much he loved her, and thanked her for all she had done for him in his life. At some point he complained that his leg was hurting, and reached down and touched the left leg. His mother said that it was the one that had been broken in three places in the accident. Stephane told his mother that he would no longer need his personal belongings, and to do whatever she wanted with them, sell them, give them away; he would no longer need them, because there was a better life coming for him. When he was finished, he told his mother that he understood everything now; and said that he would no longer bother them at home. Stephane told her that he would always love her and help her, and that he would go on to the Light as she had asked; but he wanted to talk to the others first.

His father changed places with his mother, and Stephane hugged him. It was probably more difficult for his dad, because he had been the one with him when he died, and had held him in his arms as his body grew cold. His father's childhood had been very unhappy, and he had always had a problem showing his emotions. Stephane, in his new wisdom, talked to him lovingly about this, and asked him to try to free himself of this heavy burden and to open his heart. Stephane said he had done some things which weren't always right, and asked his dad's forgiveness. Because Stephane had been in two prior accidents, something his father had not easily accepted, he wanted him to know that he hadn't done it on purpose. He said, "You know, Dad, I always loved you! We weren't always on the same wavelength because we didn't understand each other. Sometimes you would explain things to me as a parent, for my own good, but I would perceive it with the mind of a child, and I would feel you were trying to control my life, so I would refuse to take your advice. Because of the fact that I had never really found my rightful place here on earth and was unhappy, and felt rejected by everyone, I thought you were just a part of that scenario. I was beginning to understand, and have understood even more since I have been over here." His dad kissed him and told him to go to the Light!

His Aunt Gisele's turn was next. Of all his aunts, I think she was his favorite! Because of her spiritual evolution, she was the one who understood him the most during the unhappiness of his adolescent years. She stood in front of him and said, "Stephane, you know that I have always loved you very much! You must go towards the Light, towards God.

I love you, and I will always love you." She reached out to hug him, and he laid his head on her chest and said, "You are great in my heart!" Afterwards Gisele told us that this experience was very enriching for her; that it was one of the greatest moments of her life. She felt immense joy in her heart, followed by a sense of inner peace, knowing that finally her nephew Stephane was no longer "lost", but would at last be in the "Light." She said that her state of joy was comparable to what she had felt when she had given birth to each of her children, and the doctor had said, "It's a boy!" or "It's a girl!"

When Colette came up to him, Stephane was much calmer and more accepting. Smiling, he told her to continue her singing; he would hear her from up there, and he would still play with the band. He put his arms around her and said, "Au revoir, my little sister, *Coco*", which was the nickname he always had for her.

Last but not least was his buddy, Eugene! Stephane told him to keep playing his guitar, and that he would help him compose some songs. He reached out and took Eugene's right hand to squeeze it, and he felt the great strength in the handshake, as Stephane had very large hands. He said that he felt his strong life force, and knew that their friendship would transcend time and space. When Eugene moved back to his chair, Stephane was smiling and joyful.

Aware of all that was transpiring during the seance because I was not in a "deep" trance state, I was amazed at the change of energy in Stephane as his mother explained to him that he had passed over! It was like a revelation, and Stephane felt a great releasing of all the pent up emotions he had endured during that month, when he had felt so rejected because he couldn't understand why he was being ignored by his family and friends. The moment I started to feel this and could sense his real vibration without the anger and emotional pain, I realized what a beautiful soul this young man was. I then understood why he had had such a hard time focusing into the physical life. When he said good-bye to everyone and left smiling at the end of the rescue, it seemed as if he had finally found the place for which he had been searching most of his life.

His mother wanted to know when she would be able to talk to her son again, and I told her that, because of the trauma he had been through, it was important to give Stephane a much needed period of rest in the Spirit World. Because the soul connection would automatically pull him back into this dimension, I asked her to tell the whole family to leave him alone for awhile, as they had all been asking favors of him. I told her to wait three months to give him time to heal; and Stephane would let her know when he was ready.

Colette and Eugene didn't have any more manifestations in their home. However, when Colette worked near his file at the hospital, she would feel his presence strongly; and when she sang with the band she was very happy, because she knew that he was looking after her. One night Eugene was impressed to sit down and compose a song, and he knew that it was Stephane who was inspirationally giving him the words. The title is, *I Cried Tears From My Heart*, and Stephane asked that it be dedicated to his girlfriend, Linda.

After the rescue work, the house warmed up immediately. They never again felt the bone chilling cold and the slight breezes they had experienced before, and Stephane no longer visited his relatives' homes.

Planning to use this wonderful story for a chapter in my book, I asked each one who had been a part of it, to share their personal experiences as they had lived them. Gisele, Colette and Eugene put everything on paper for me, but I decided to interview Gaetane. It would take too long for her to write it all, and we always pick up the emotional side of an experience during a taped interview. A few weeks later, knowing I was leaving for several months in Florida, during which time I planned to finish my book, I found time to interview Gaetane on the 22nd of December. During that time I had felt Stephane around occasionally; but would just send him love, without opening myself up to him. Gaetane and I chatted awhile, as I felt there were some things she needed to talk about, and then we got on with the interview, which took about an hour, after which I immediately had to leave. As I got ready to leave, I sensed Stephane around. At the same time his mother looked at me and said, "It suddenly got very cold all around me." I told her that Stephane was with us, and left. As I got into the car, he was with me instantly. Sensing his emotions so strongly, I wanted to cry as I felt his disappointment at not having been able to talk to his mother! I told him that I was sorry that I didn't have time now, but that I would call and tell her when I got home. That night I called and gave her his message: "He would be with her and the family at Christmas!"

I called her to say good-bye the day before I left, and asked how her Christmas had been. She had spent it at home with her family, because she was taking care of her elderly mother who had come out of the hospital for a few days. Gaetane was very joyful, and shared with me the experiences she had had on Christmas Eve, when the French Canadians always celebrate the holiday with Midnight Mass and a large meal at 2:00 a.m.! She was in the kitchen, and suddenly heard a noise on the patio. She thought, "the cat is out there and wants to come in", and she opened the door to call him; but he was not there. It happened a second time a few minutes later, and the same thing occurred. There was no one there! But as she walked back into the kitchen, something told her to look at the clock. As she did, she noticed that the hands were on *1:05*, the exact moment Stephane had died three months before. When she went into the living room, she found the cat asleep on the sofa. Trying to make this Christmas celebration as normal as possible for the family, after the meal they put the music on and started to dance. Gaetane felt Stephane's presence so strongly that she knew he was dancing with her at times, for she could feel the cool breeze close to her. She mentioned this to a young friend of Stephane's, who had been staying with them for a week, and he said as a joke, "Aren't you going to dance with me, Stephane?". Immediately the cold air surrounded him so swiftly that he nearly freaked out, much to everyone's enjoyment!

While I was writing Stephane's story, I felt him around me often. When he came in to say hello, his energy was so powerful that even I got the shivers from head to toe. I shared my writing with my friend Mary, who manages the complex where I live. As I finished a part of each chapter, I would take it to her to read, as she is very open and has many Spiritual gifts. While I was talking about Stephane with Mary, he often manifested, and the hair would stand up all over both of our bodies at the same time. We would look at each other and laugh, acknowledging his presence with love.

A beautiful picture of Stephane, one of the last ones taken before he passed, sat on the desk beside my computer during the time I spent writing this story. Gaetane gave it to me as a souvenir of my work with them. He often came in to talk for a few moments, and I could sense that he was very happy where he was. But Stephane's energy is so powerful, and he has evolved so quickly in the Spirit World, that he is beginning to feel that it is time to get on with his work of helping others, which he was unable to finish on earth. I feel that one of the ways Stephane would like to perform this task, and he came in and confirmed it for me with great joy, was in being able to help the people who would read his story, and would like to connect with him *soulwise*. This may help those of you who are deeply touched by Stephane's experience. Some of you may have had a child "return home to the Spirit World" at a young age and you have never accepted their leaving! This is because you didn't understand that our children are only loaned to us from God; and, as the soul, we choose the time when we will make the return trip to our "real home" in the World of Spirit. If you choose to connect with Stephane on a love vibration, I am sure there is much he can do to help you Spiritually and otherwise, if what you are asking is for your highest good!

Last Picture of Stephane – 1991

Chapter Eleven

THE LIBERATION AND ASCENSION
OF JASON

In April of 1991, Michelyne came to spend two weeks with me before my return to Canada. On Thursday evening, we decided to go out to a restaurant for dinner, and afterwards we walked around the shopping center, looking in the store windows. In one of those windows, a poster of a missing twelve year old boy caught my eye. I felt drawn to his eyes; and, as I did, I psychically felt a shovel hit me on the top of my head, and I was falling to the ground. For a brief moment I pictured a man holding the shovel, and then it was gone. I knew immediately that the boy was no longer living in the physical, and what I had felt had something to do with the way he had died. I looked at the poster and noticed that there was only the name and phone number of the detective in charge of the case. I felt sick and tried to put it out of my mind, all the while sending love and Light to this young soul.

The next day was Friday. I planned to attend a meditation course with an organization with which I wanted to connect, as I felt that their teachings were the same as mine. I worked on my book for several hours, and in the afternoon I started to feel strange; but I was too busy to think much about it. The sensation got worse, until I finally had to stop what I was doing. I was feeling very confused, and sick from head to toe, as if every part of my body were out of kilter! Miche was getting ready to go to the meditation with me, and I went to talk to her. I told her how I was feeling, and explained that I had never felt anything like this in my life! She advised me to meditate on it and tune into what was happening. Sitting in my usual meditation chair in my room, I immediately saw the young boy whose picture I had seen the day before on the poster. He was standing right beside me! Then I knew that when I had connected with him through his eyes, he had been drawn to me for the help he needed. I had never felt so much confusion in anyone as I did in this soul, and I felt blessed that he had come to me for the help he needed to go into the Light. I talked to him lovingly, told him his suffering was over now, and that he would be with God. I visualized the Light in a corner of my room, and asked him to walk into it, assuring him that there would be people there to help him. This he did, and I was very happy to psychically see him ascend.

Afterwards I sat there and cried. I could emotionally feel what his parents were going through, and I would have given anything to have been able to let them know that their son was alright and no longer suffering. But how do you call an unknown detective in a police station, and explain to him over the phone what I have shared with you? The only things I remembered about the poster was that he was a very handsome boy, that he had lived in what I thought was a midwestern state, and that there was such a huge reward, that I wondered if an extra zero hadn't been added by mistake.

A few days later I was busy packing and closing my apartment, preparing for my return to Canada for the summer months. I often sent him loving thoughts to help him adjust to his new life. With my knowledge of the afterlife,

I knew that because of the trauma caused to the soul from his premature and violent passing, he would be in a place of rest and healing for several months. I always tell those who call me when they have lost loved ones, to give them time to heal and adjust and not try to contact them for a few months. They will make their presence known when they are ready.

When I returned to Florida six months later, I went to the same store to see if the flyer was still in the window; but the company had gone out of business, and a new occupant was in its place. As I was writing about this experience in March, 1992, I felt the same vibration as I had that day, and knew that the same young soul had come in to touch with me once again. I still felt a little confusion and a great sadness in him, which made me feel that the family had not received the answers they were seeking. They were not at the point of acceptance that they were blessed to have had him for the short number of years they did. He will stay around to help them the best he can, but he must be permitted to continue his soul growth on the other side. This can only occur when the people closest to him on this side accept that he is in the Kingdom of God now, even though they don't understand how or why something like this could happen!

I surrounded him with love and asked him to come back when I meditated that night and we would talk. I would try to help him understand what happened, and release all the negative energy around this lifetime. I also wanted him to know that he would have the privilege of coming back again in another lifetime, when the time is right, and should he so desire.

On September 16, 1992, I was again in florida and my daughter Lisa was visiting me from Canada. I was out that evening and, as I returned home and walked into the living room, she mentioned that the program on television was on kidnapped children. I glanced at the screen and I immediately recognized the case they were discussing. It was the boy I had seen on the poster in the store window a year and a half before. I vividly remembered his face, and the amount of the reward coincided with the large amount about which I had remarked before.

I felt very sad that his parents had never found out what had happened to him, and were still waiting. As I sat in the chair, feeling very emotional, I got the shivers from head to toe, and the hair stood up on my arms, as it usually does when a spirit approaches me in my capacity as a medium. As usual, I opened myself to my connection with the Spirit World, to see why this soul was trying to make its presence known to me, and what I could do to help. I immediately recognized the same beautiful soul who had touched with me twice before. His confusion was completely gone. Before me was a very wise soul who was at peace with himself through the acquiring of a great deal of spiritual growth. He gently conveyed the message that he wanted me to let his parents know that he was alright! Feeling guilty about my lack of action, and realizing the suffering his family had been through during those eighteen months, I made him a promise. This time I would do something about it!

When I stepped into the living room, they had almost finished reporting on his disappearance. Before I had time to write down the 800 number flashing on the screen for his case, they had changed to the story of another child. Lisa wrote down the telephone number given at the end of the program which we could call to get a copy of all that had transpired. I was sure that it would contain the phone number I needed to make contact with someone working on this case.

Upon calling, I found it would take a week to receive this information, and I thought that there must be a way to get it sooner. I mentioned it to Lori, one of my young students who has awakened beautifully in a very short period through taking my development classes. We have a strong "soul connection"; she senses when I am going through emotional upheavals, and calls to see if I am alright. Having lived in Florida for twelve years, Lori was much more knowledge-able than I about who to contact; as I knew I couldn't go through regular channels. She found the numbers for a missing children's hotline, and for "America's Most Wanted", which gives advice in these cases. It was 9:00 P.M. and she sat down to read, expecting to give me the phone numbers the next day. Immediately she heard a "dry cracking sound" in a corner, which she recognized from my teachings as the sound of a spirit coming in. She felt the cold around her and the hair stood up all over her body, and she distinctly heard a voice in her mind say: *"MAKE THE PHONE CALL NOW!"* She could see a young boy in her mind's eye, and knew that it was my little friend Jason (not his real name), refusing to wait any longer.

The next day I called America's Most Wanted and asked where I could get a copy of the flyer on a missing child. She told me to go to the nearest police station and they would give me one. I was hoping to find an understanding person, someone who was open to this type of phenomena. On arriving there I was told that the lady in charge of missing persons was very ill and could not talk to me. However, they did give me a photocopy of the flyer.

I meditated on how I should proceed with relaying my information. I wanted at least one person with whom I could relate spiritually, and who could understand a little something about "where I was coming from!"

Meanwhile, Jason was always around to remind me that he was still waiting for me to keep my promise. I felt that he had a special love bond with his mom, and he wanted her to stop worrying about him. When I felt him close and I knew he wanted to talk, I would telepathically chat with him, reassuring him that I was really trying to get the proof as quickly as I could to take to his family. Several times when I was sharing this experience with different friends, the hair would stand up on our arms. We would laugh and welcome him. I could hear him say, "Yes, I'm right here, and I'm still waiting!"

My search started by trying to find a deep trance medium through whom Jason could manifest, give his own proof of survival, and any other details he could about his death. After many phone calls, I realized that there are not many "deep trance" medium anymore! This is because the energy on the planet has changed from the density it was for eons to a much lighter energy. The vibratory rate on our planet has been raised several times over the past fifteen years. Mankind is moving from the third dimension into the fourth dimension, and the planet is being "Spiritualized", as our Creator prepares, **"To bring Heaven down on earth, as it was originally meant to be!"** Therefore, there are more "mental mediums". This means that we repeat what we are being given telepathically by the Spirit World, or we are in a state of altered consciousness, and aware of what is coming through us.

The 5th of October 1992 was my first meeting with Jim Gordon. Because I don"t like to "feed" information to a trance medium before they go into a trance state,I did not tell him what I was looking for. My philosopher guide came in first, and we talked for about twenty minutes about all kinds of things that concerned me. Then it was my beloved *Strong Bow's* turn to chat. He answered all my questions about what was happening in my life, and put my fears to rest with his loving advice. I had hoped that Jason would be able to come in for a minute at least, to make his presence known, but instead, Jim snapped out of his trance state so suddenly that he himself was shocked! I told him, "That was beautiful, but it wasn't exactly what I was looking for!" He asked what I needed; that perhaps he could help me clairvoyantly. After coming out of the trance state, a medium is still in the energy for a short period of time, and can receive many answers. I told him I was looking for information about a missing person, and gave him only the first name, with no other details.

After telling me the boy was fourteen or fifteen years old, he said: "I'm sorry, but this young boy is no longer in the physical", which I knew of course, as I had done a soul rescue on him. He went on to say that he had passed in a tragic way and that it had been a violent death. He gave me more details about how it had happened, and then went on to give me a description of the murderer. He said he was:

1. very roguish, rough looking type of person;
2. has a straggly short beard;
3. has a problem with alcohol or drug addiction of some type;
4. his residence is in the same area as Jason's family, but he goes away to work for months at a time and then he returns;
5. wears "pendleton" shirts (plaid type worn by lumbermen or outdoor workers etc.), and a knitted cap (toque);
6. he doesn't always work in the same place; "I see nature, and moose...";

7. he could be as young as the mid-thirties but felt he was probably older;

8. the boy died and is buried way up in northern Minnesota somewhere.

While chatting with Jim, he immediately threw his right hand up and said: "Wait a minute, I'm getting something else!" He started writing in the air in huge letters with his index finger, repeating them as he was writing: "C... H... I... S... H... O... L... M... Chisholm, Minnesota!" He was shocked and said: "God! I've never been to Minnesota! I don't know if this place even exists, but I feel it's in the northern part of the State. This is the area where the body is buried, or where it all happened!"

I was with my friend Bonnie, and we went back to her house in West Palm Beach to look at an atlas to see if there was such a place in Minnesota. There it was, in the northeastern part of the State; and the map showed drawings of trees, which signify an area where there are forests!

Lori was meditating a week later, when Jason's face appeared in front of her. This is the vision she was given, and I quote: "I saw a double barrel shotgun, heard the pin being pulled back, and both bullets were fired. Then I saw the figure of a person laying in front of a car off the road which looked like a turnpike or interstate, because I could see the car lights whizzing by. The person laying on the ground was a young boy, but I knew it was not Jason. The man holding the gun was wearing what looked like a red and black plaid flannel shirt and blue jeans, with brown hiking boots. He was wearing a black knitted cap rolled up, sort of like a type of ski cap. He had a short "scraggly looking" beard, and I'm not sure if he had a mustache, but I think he did. The man looked to be in his thirties, and he was standing in front of what I felt was an older model Ford station wagon. The body was laying in front of him, and he was looking at it while holding the gun. A few seconds later, I saw Jason sitting on an unmarked grave in a heavily wooded area".

Lori, having only a month's experience in my classes, did not know how to interpret the vision she had been given by Jason; but I knew immediately that he wanted her to get the message to me that this man was still killing young boys.

It was a very stressful few weeks, for I wanted to find the right person. It wasn't exactly what I had hoped it would be; but after consultations with three different mediums, I had enough information to start. I couldn't make Jason wait any longer.

As I do every day during the months I am in Florida, I went for breakfast that morning at a little coffee shop called The Chemist Shop, on Las Olas Boulevard, in Fort Lauderdale. I was trying to get my thoughts straight as to how I would write all the information I had for the police. Suddenly I felt Jason's presence right beside me, and he mentally showed me the numbers 5-7. I immediately knew that he wanted me to tell the police that this man had killed between five and seven other boys!

Saturday, October 10th, I finally made the first phone call. At 2:15 I sat down to dial the number. I was praying his father or mother wouldn't answer, for what I had to tell them was not something I could explain over the phone. I was almost relieved when there was no answer, and I decided to wait until Monday to try again.

On Monday I dialed the number in Minnesota again. A man answered, and I explained a little about what I had called to tell them. (It is not easy to explain this to someone over the phone, although I can usually pick up immediately on their degree of Spiritual awareness.) He asked me to wait, and I felt that he passed me through to someone else, although he said he was the same person. I liked his vibration, and I did'nt feel any negativity towards what I was saying, just the opposite. He seemed very open, in spite of the fact that he admitted knowing nothing about soul rescue work, or even the fact that it existed. I gave him the details of my meeting, and the information I had received from my friend Jim Gordon of West Palm Beach. (I consider Jim one of the best trance mediums I have found so far.) I told him I had more details, but had not had time to put them on my computer. Because I would be away for a three-day Spiritual conference, I would send them to him on my return.

October 17th was the day I finally decided to keep my promise, and send to the Deputy Sheriff in charge of the case the information I had acquired over the past few weeks. I felt that some of the info from the first medium was possibly less accurate than what came through Jim, but it contained a lot of "trivia", which can sometimes help identify the soul, because it can be things that only someone who knows them well, would recognize.

I sent them a resume about myself and my Spiritual work, and explained about my twenty-five year business background as well. I told them about my manuscript, which was at a publisher's at that point, and included part of the chapter which contained the soul rescue of Jason. I wrote: "Jason has a very important message that I promised I would get to his mom and dad for him. He is in the Spirit World, and is alright, and to stop worrying about him! I have to depend on you to see that this message is relayed to them in the most humane and loving way possible, along with a copy of part of the chapter of my book that contains his story.

If they wish to get in touch with me, I ask that you give them my phone number. Working with families who have been through the same tragic experience as they have is part of my Spiritual work, and I have given, and am still giving, many people the proof, that their loved ones are not dead, but have only moved on to a higher plane of existence.

"The fact that Jason brought me the message that this murderer is still taking the lives of other young boys is also an indication that the police must work very hard to catch him. I know that Jason will do what he can to help you from where he is, because he warned me this morning that this person has killed at least five to seven others. I also distinctly heard him say "Nebraska", which gave me the impression that there may be some from that State as well. Perhaps you can check with the police there; you might find they have had similar unsolved cases.

"I will keep up the search for more clues. Now that I know there are other boys besides Jason, I feel more implicated than just trying to keep a promise to transmit his message to his mom and dad. I know the potential I have for this work. If this person has ever been arrested, I could possibly identify him for you through your "mug shot" books.

"If I can be of help in any way, please don't hesitate to contact me."

Jason was around me often, especially during the times when I was doing work regarding his case. He would always let me know when he came in by making the hair stand up all over my body, and I would welcome him. Now and then I would reach out, throw my arms around him, laughingly give him a big hug and say, "How are you doing, sweetie?"

I was getting a little discouraged and sometimes felt like giving up, but I knew I had to keep trying. On October 26th, I decided to visit Jim Gordon one more time.

Strong Bow came in first this time. When he asked me if I had any questions, I said: "I want to know about this young boy on whom I did a soul rescue a year and a half ago. I want some proof for his family that he is really in the Spirit World, and I wondered if he could come through for himself."

Strong Bow

– We will try, but I do not think that he will be able to tell you much. (He gave some details of what had happened which I prefer not to describe here). It is a horrible thing to contemplate, and sometimes truth is hard to face, but it's better to face facts than to try to avoid unpleasantness. This young boy, who has such a small amount of karma to pay because he is so young; the negative karma is already gone, and he is a free spirit. I think it is not wise to keep reminding him of his tragic ending to his earthly life. He is very aware of Spiritual things of his true life, but I understand that those he has left behind have not reached this point of enlightenment as he has. They are still dwelling, and it's understandable, on his fate, always hoping against hope that he will return. But time has wonderful healing qualities to it, and we never will forget this boy. His family will never forget; but with each passing day, the pain is a little less, and this is what is called acceptance. Oh, if we would only learn to accept! Then we don't have to experience the thing again! (Karma involved in the acceptance.) But to deny something, and keep denying it, only keeps the wound open. We find that denial does no good because it is reality. So we pray not so much for the boy, who needs our prayers less, but for those he has left behind, because they need our prayers more. I can tell you that if you continue to do the things you are doing on behalf of other people, you will begin receiving more and more accurate information through your own abilities. This is in part what your work is to be during the next few years. It is to do not only soul rescue for those who have come to our world, but also to bring to justice those who have caused such misery for the ones who have been left behind. It is easy for many to say, "Well, let us forget it; it is over, it is done with, let us go on! God is the one who judges." The Bible says **"vengeance is mine sayeth the Lord"**; not vengeance of fire and brimstone, but justice; obeying the laws of the land, and not to allow someone to escape from their crime, although we know that there is no escape, because the long hand of the Lords of Karma bring each one of us to the final mirror where we look at ourselves. And we are not judged by some strange god; we are our own judge, for the mirror is the greatest camera, and we are all the photographers.

I then asked him to tell me something about my Spiritual work. Because it concerns soul rescue, I thought it was important to share part of it with you.

Strong Bow
– You see, you have many talents; healing of course, but the soul rescue work which is very delicate, and many who do not know the basic laws of travelling into some of those lower astral worlds should not play with those things! But you have the **Light** and you have the understanding, so there is no danger for you. People should learn that no matter how generous their hearts and their thoughts may be, they must be realistic and practical. This is a beautiful city! Beautiful homes in a beautiful city! Beautiful people in beautiful homes; but like all beautiful cities, there is a dark place too! There are those

who live in darkness. Their thoughts are of crime, of lust, of addictions; they do not live in beautiful places. They live only to the level of their thought, their consciousness. And so it is in the astral world! You come many times with us to beautiful places, to listen to the words of great ones, to see and to listen to the great orchestras, to the great voices of all times, to see a scientist, to hear explorers, to hear all of these people, philosophers as well as some theologians. (*Strong Bow* was explaining about how they come and get me during the sleep state.) But there is a dark place in the astral, where those who have died violent unexpected deaths, through accident, murder, suicide, war; these young people whose bodies are blown to pieces, they're not prepared for this world! They walk in a grey zone looking for some **Light**. They're not evil, they are not bad, but they are lost! That is where those like yourself can go and talk to them of the Light. Get them to speak of someone they love who is already on that side of life. That person then gravitates to that Light. This is rescue work. But back to what I was saying, those people who are not knowledgeable of this work should not play with it.

I asked him if he thought I would receive any answer from the police.

Strong Bow
– I strongly believe that you will. It may not be a letter of acceptance, but I believe that it will be something courteous, an acknowledgement. Times are changing very quickly and people in law enforcement have had too many true, correct psychic people give them accurate information for them to dismiss it any more! Publicly

they deny it, but privately they believe it. But you will hear from them.

Can you tell me if what someone picked up is true, that this man had also killed other children?

Strong Bow

  – It is sad to say, but that is true; Jason is not the first. Unless and until this man is captured, Jason will not be the last! That is why I say that soul rescue is wonderful, but bringing to justice this person is equally important. It is through the information you get from various sources, and supplying it to the authorities, that this can come to pass. The only drawback is time! As time goes on, less and less interest is shown because the police have other cases to work on.

Will they give the information to his family as I asked? The important thing is that Jason wants them to know that he is alright.

Strong Bow

  – I believe it has already been discussed. And he is alright! You are like a mother, you cared for him. It's true, when a person comes to this world, in the beginning they are like a baby. They want to know what has happened to them. So he feels like you are a mother to him, a Spiritual mother. He knows where he is now, and he's full of curiosity, loves his school work, loves to learn. He's learning everything here he would have learned in earth school, only so much more.

When *Strong Bow* was finished, my philosopher guide came in and talked for several minutes. At some point he said that Jason was with them and would do his best to come through, but he was very nervous, and was standing drawing circles on the floor with his foot. When he was through he said, "Well, I'm going to just step to the side; I don't want to leave Jason alone." It took about a minute and then this little voice said:

Jason
 – Hi!

Carole
 – Hi, Jason!

Jason
 – BOY, THAT WAS A FAST TRIP; IT WAS JUST LIKE BEING ON A JET! ALL OF A SUDDEN I'M HERE!

Carole
 – That's wonderful.

Jason
 – THEY TOLD ME NOT TO BE AFRAID TO SAY THANK YOU.

Carole
 – You're welcome, Sweetie.

Jason
 – I SURE LIKE YOU VERY MUCH!

Carole
 – I love you too.

Jason
 – I LIKE WHERE YOU LIVE TOO. I LOVE TO GO BY THE WATER.

Carole
 – (laughing) You're there often.

Jason
 – YES, I AM. I HAVE A LOT OF FUN THERE.

Carole

    – I know you do.

Jason

    – (pause) I DON'T KNOW WHAT TO SAY!

Carole

    – Is there anything you want to say to your mom and dad? Do you have a message for them?

Jason

    – THAT I LOVE THEM; AND I'M ALRIGHT! THEY WON'T SEE ME AGAIN LIKE THEY SAW ME BEFORE (in a physical body), BUT SOMEDAY THEY'LL SEE ME. I JUST WANT THEM NOT TO CRY ANY MORE.

Carole

    – Are you making your presence known to them. Are you working on that, Babe?

Jason

    – I'M TRYING TO. I DON'T HURT AND I'M NOT AFRAID... AND I DON'T REMEMBER! I DON'T REMEMBER VERY MUCH... JUST A MAN... HE HAD A TERRIBLE SMELL ON HIM... I THOUGHT MAYBE HE DIDN'T TAKE A BATH, BUT HE DID! HE HAD SOMETHING IN A BOTTLE... OH! HE PUT IT ALL OVER HIS FACE AND HIS NECK... AND IT SMELLED CHEAP... BUT I JUST REMEMBER HIM IN THE LITTLE OLD PICKUP TRUCK, SMELLING SO BAD; AND THEN I DON'T REMEMBER ANYTHING ELSE!

Carole

    – It's good that you don't remember, but if you ever have anything for me...

Jason

    – THE REVEREND TOLD ME NOT EVEN TO TRY TO REMEMBER. HE SAID, "WHAT'S DONE IS DONE, NOW

LET'S GET ON!" HE'S ONE OF MY FRIENDS THAT I
FOUND OVER HERE; HE TAKES CARE OF A LOT OF
KIDS... A LOT OF KIDS. HE'S A NICE MAN... HE'S OLD
TOO... BUT HE'S FULL OF PEP.

Carole

– That's great.

Jason

– I LOVE YOU!

Carole

– I love you too!

Jason

– AND I'LL KEEP RAPPING ON THE WINDOW PANE.

Carole

– (laughing) O.K. keep rapping; come in anytime you
want to.

Jason

– BYE FOR NOW!

Carole

– Bye, honey!

After Jim came out of his trance state, I asked if he could
get anything else through his clairvoyance. This is what he
saw:

1. The first thing I see is a tree with a big branch; a
low branch growing out of it, and there is a rope at the end
of it, and an old rubber tire is tied to it. There are several
kids playing around there, and I feel it is a place where kids
often played. I feel that there is a man that these kids were
accustomed to seeing. He didn't appear to be a stranger to
them, because I don't see them running away from him; he's
a very friendly person. I see an old grey pickup truck with
a lot of gardening tools and dirt in the back... rakes, shovels,

hoes and one of those old fashioned push type lawn mowers. There's no writing on the side of it, but it is an old, old truck. This man has a baseball cap on. I put him to be about 40 or 45 years old; he's not an old man nor a young man. He has a couple of cases of soda pop and he gives these out to the children. I don't like this person; I don't like this man at all!

2. This tree is at the end of a vacant lot, and there is a house on either side. I see flocks of pigeons flying around in circles. Their coop is nearby, and there are fifteen or twenty pigeons flying in a flock, very close to the ground. Very near to this vacant lot are two houses, one on each side. Quite near there is an open playground near a school which needs to be rebuilt; it is so old that it really needs to be demolished. I feel like this boy and his friends played there sometimes. The kids liked the empty lot better because they would pull up long clumps of grass and throw it at each other.

3. This boy was taken a long, long way from that neighborhood before he died, but I believe that the man is back in that area. I feel he did a lot of work in that neighborhood and that he lived around there. From the appearance of the truck and all the gardening tools in the back, I would assume that he did gardening or landscaping work. It seems to be a nice area; and he doesn't seem to fit as one who would live there, but he's there a lot. And those pigeons... I'm seeing them again, and they are swooping very low, as if they are getting ready to go into their pigeon house, or whatever they call it. The baseball cap he has on has a blue star on it, right in the front. There is some other decoration or insignia around it, but it is a five pointed star. It's very dirty and sweaty looking.

On November 14, I wrote another letter to the Deputy Sheriff, and sent off all the new information I had been able to acquire. During the next month Jason was often in and out. But as we approached the holiday season, he came less and less. I felt that he was spending a lot of time in his home to help his family get through another Christmas, with the sadness of not knowing what had happened to him.

I never received an acknowledgement from those working on the case or anyone else, as *Strong Bow* had thought I would. So I just gave up my search, for it was costing me a lot of time and money. (I had to pay the mediums myself, as none of them work for free, even if it is for something important like this.) But when I make a promise to a spirit, I will do all I can to keep that promise; I knew there was nothing more I could do without some co-operation from others.

On March 16th 1993, I was going through some trauma in my personal life, and feeling as if I needed some insight from *Strong Bow*. I headed up to West Palm Beach to see Jim Gordon for a reading. *Strong Bow* consoled me and was able to help me put my life back in perspective. He gave me much information on all the new doors which he said would be opening in my life on my return from my trip to visit my family and friends in Canada. At the end of the reading I asked him how Jason was doing, and if it would be possible for him to come through and talk to me again some time. He said: "It is possible, but this child is deeply emerged in studies. He is learning the things he was not able to learn on the earth plane, but also Spiritual things. He is very interested in geography, and he's learning the location of all the different countries. He's learning about the history of each country, and this is fascinating for him. He was deprived of this opportunity while in the body, but he's also growing Spiritually. This fine boy is going to be a fine young man, who in turn will serve many people. You have much for which to be thankful; you were involved in rescuing this child from the pits of confusion and darkness, and he will be eternally grateful. One day, a young man will come and speak with you from the Spirit World, and you will find that it is he.

I said that I had never heard anything from the police or his family...

Strong Bow
— And perhaps you will not! They have their own way of accepting these things... but you've done for that one who is the most important, Jason; the rest... the seeds are planted, maybe they will come to fruition... maybe they will not, at least in this lifetime. But for you, that is not important, for your role as the sower is finished as far as they are concerned. You've done your part; now you will reap what you have sown.

Chapter Twelve

MY BELOVED FRANÇOIS GOES HOME AT LAST

This is not a chapter on soul rescue, but I believe it is one of the most important ones in the whole book and is very dear to my heart. I feel very blessed in having been able to share this experience with François and his family, for it is truly a story of love between a mother and her son. They had known each other from past lives, and came together in this lifetime to help each other grow spiritually and acquire a great inner faith. I don't believe there is a greater learning experience for a mother than to lose a child, born of our flesh and raised with love, only to have him taken from us at a very young age. Without faith nothing makes sense, for we always wonder why God is punishing us! But when we understand that karma is the only answer in these experiences, even though it doesn't make it any easier, at least we accept that it is happening for a reason. From the very beginning we must accept that our children do not belong to us, but are souls who have chosen to come through us for the experiences **they** need in this lifetime. They have their own karmic patterns to work out, and their own learning lessons; we should try to see everything in their lives from that point of view. Knowing this doesn't help much when tragedies occur unexpectedly; because, being in the physical body as we are, we must work it all out emotionally. I have come to understand that we are on this planet to evolve our emotional bodies, and we must have these experiences in order to receive the soul growth for which we incarnated.

It is also the story of a wonderful young man who was a very advanced soul; and what really happens when we are *prepared* for our return to the World of Spirit, accepting with joy that we are really only "Going Home" after a long trip filled with trials and tribulations. This is the realization we must all come to at some point. Everyone must understand that this life is only temporary and that our "real home" is in the World of Spirit. We are "Spirit" first and foremost. But we must also understand that we are responsible for all our acts, and must answer to the law of cause and effect both in this lifetime and from past lives.

The first time Nicole came to me for a reading was in 1983. She was married to a local boy and had two children, both boys. We had been living in the same small town for many years. Her husband had been ill for several years with kidney problems, and was now traveling to a hospital near Montreal for dialysis treatments three times a week. Nicole and her husband were clients in our insurance brokerage business from the very beginning, so I would see her now and then.

Nicole was going through a very strong emotional situation in her personal life. She heard about what I was doing, and thought I might be able to help her. The reading helped clarify many things, and gave her a new perspective on what life was really all about. During my readings I work with natural, spiritual and karmic law. In her case she was living a strong karmic pattern with a certain person who had come into her life, and with whom there was a strong karmic tie from a past life. It is difficult for others to understand the strong bond between two people, and the loving friendship that can exist. They were being judged by many who had nothing better to do, and it was causing dissension in the family. During the reading, I explained all about karma and why this strong bond existed. Spirit showed me that this man had been her husband in a past life, and her two children had been with them at that time. Putting things in perspective for her in a Spiritual sense helped her to get on with her life. She was able to raise herself above all the gossip, knowing that she was exactly where she was supposed to be to work out this karmic pattern from long ago.

At the end of the reading she talked about her son François, and the great affinity they had with each other. From the time François was very young, he had been saying all kinds of strange things! When he was about twelve, he said: "Mom, you know I believe in reincarnation!" She was surprised, for they had never discussed things like this at home and they were devout Catholics. Nicole had even been working at the presbytery as secretary to the local priest for many years. She then told me that François had told her on several occasions that he knew he was going to die before he was twenty. I advised her to tell him to stop this immediately, because the subconscious mind, being so strong, could program his death.

Nicole decided to take the session of my beginners' course which was starting soon, because she realized she needed help with her Spirituality, which was beginning to unfold. About a month into the course, Nicole called to tell me that she would miss a class; François had to go to the hospital for some tests for a cyst or tumor which had appeared in the neck area. Later she advised me that the tumor was malignant. It was then that I understood that he had not "programmed" his departure from the earth plane, but that he was a very evolved soul who had the inner knowledge that he had only come to the planet for a short sojourn.

Having already started her own Spiritual pathway at that point, Nicole was able to help François understand what was happening to him, having had her own proof through my course that life continues after the so-called state of "death". There followed many hours of discussion between mother and son, who were so much in harmony that they could read each other's mind, amusing them both greatly. They discussed all the aspects of what life was in reality, and his mother always marveled at his universal and Spiritual knowledge!

François went to a hospital in Montreal for a short period, and then came home to continue his treatments at the local hospital. There came a day when he had a decision to make: to continue taking his chemotherapy treatments, which made him ill for several days each month and would prolong his life for a year or two, or stop them and shorten his time left on earth!

He discussed the situation with his parents. His mother told him that the decision was his alone because, like every human being, his life belonged only to him. On his next trip to the hospital, he insisted on the doctor doing more tests to see if there were any changes. After viewing the X-rays, he had to admit that the tumor had not shrunk, in fact, François thought it had gotten a little larger. It was at that moment when he made his decision to stop all treatment, much to the disappointment of his doctor who told him he was committing suicide!

To make his time left as happy as possible, his parents bought him his first car. He had a girlfriend and was trying not to get too attached to her, because he knew that in a short time he would have to leave her. Nicole called me from time to time, keeping me informed of his progress. She said: "He's wonderful! Do you know what he's doing now? He's preparing his funeral; the music and everything!" She said he wanted to come and talk with me, and asked if I could meet with him.

François came the following week, and we went into my center, where we could talk quietly. He was magnificent! I knew I had before me a young body, with a great soul and a lot of wisdom. He shared with me the fact that the moment he decided to terminate his treatment, he felt a great peace in his soul and an immense inner joy! These were his words: "My physical body is finished, and I won't be able to use it anymore to help others as I wanted; so I've decided to go back to the other side, because I can help a lot more people from there!"

He also told me of his desire to give his mother a message just before the end. I assured him that God would surely grant this wish! He asked his mother to take my advanced courses, because "otherwise you won't be able to understand me when I talk to you from over there."

I asked him why he didn't write his own "Homily" and we could tape it to play during his funeral. In this way he could possibly help many people understand in reality what life and death are. The following is what he wrote:

"I would like my family and my friends who are here to be able to share my joy with me today! Many of you will say that my suffering is finished! But when we understand that the suffering, if suffering there is, takes us to the door of the Kingdom of God, it is easily accepted!

"My 19 years on Earth were lived fully, because I was blessed with good parents and a brother. Also, many friends

*of my own age, that I would have liked to make understand that **Divine Love** exists, that they too may be able to find the Eternal Light that I found in the last year of my physical life .*

"To my beloved Mother I give my eternal gratitude for all of the love that she gave me! During this last year, she shared with me each important moment with a smile, and sometimes with tears, the joy that I felt, in spite of her Mother's heart often breaking, knowing that she would greatly miss my physical presence. But she also has found the Light, and she knows that our separation is only for a short period, and is simply an Au Revoir."

He used to drop in and see me often, and we would go down to my center and sit down to chat. He would share with me all that was happening, and tell me how much he was enjoying his life. He would zip around town in his car visiting all of his friends, and would sometimes go hunting when the season was right. He would tell me how much he would like to be able to influence his friends to get off drugs and take responsibility for their lives, and would always take the opportunity to talk to them about this subject. François was greatly admired for the way he was handling his life and forthcoming death, and it was a lesson to many people, both young and old!

I decided to call Pierre Milot, the man with the T.V. program on parapsychology on which I had made an appearance a few weeks before. I asked him if he would be interested in doing a program with François and his mother. I felt that this beautiful story would help many people who were going through the same experience, and were afraid of dying. Also those people who, due to their fears, were not living their lives to the fullest, because they did not understand what transition is, but know that they will eventually have to face it.

The three of us did the program. Pierre interviewed me first, and I introduced François, who sat with us and discussed his experience as if it were the most natural thing in the world, which it is. His mother then shared her side of the story, and how she was coping with it all. It was beautiful to see the loving interaction between François and his mother, and their acceptance of the experience as a Spiritual growing lesson for them both. Needless to say, Pierre received a vast number of letters and calls following this program.

My advanced class always included a seance, and one day François asked if he could sit in on my class that night. I accepted immediately, as I thought it might help him in some way. During the seance, Rose went into trance, and we did several soul rescue cases through her. She always worked in a very deep state of trance and had no knowledge whatsoever of what was happening *through* her. When it was time for her to come out of her deep state, I always watched very closely to see that she came back without problems because Spirit always brought through some tough cases when she was working. As she was slowly coming back, I realized that another spirit was coming through her. I welcomed this soul, and he said his name was Sebastian, "and that he had come to talk to his brother, François!"

Aware that this spirit had come to talk to him, François asked him what he had to say. He said: "I am here to tell you that it is not quite time for you to come and join us, as your physical body is not used enough yet; but in a short period, it shall be so. We want you to know that when that time arrives, we shall be waiting for you." He then asked François if he had anything to ask him; and for the first time since I had known this young man, I heard a slight sob. He answered, "I would like you to help me with three things.

First, that I be able to make the transition in my own bed, not a hospital environment. Second, that you help me for the pain. Third, that I may be able to give my mother a message at the moment of my passing!" Sebastian said that this would be done, and that he would see him soon.

After the seance I asked him if his mother had ever had a miscarriage, and he said yes. I explained that the child must have been a boy and that he had grown up in the Spirit World, coming in to help the family when needed, as often happens with miscarriages and abortions.

A few months later, Irene Griffey came to spend a week with me for her twice yearly visit to my center. François attended one of the seances and brought a young girl with him. Her fifteen year old sister had been killed during the summer, while crossing the road in our small town. Having a hard time recovering from the shock of losing her sister, François thought that she might come through to talk to her, and help her accept her passing. The sister came through Irene and formed her face, which was easily recognizable by those who knew her, and talked to her. She was greatly consoled because she now had the proof of survival. She accepted that her sister was alive and well, living in another dimension, and that it was possible for her to communicate with her telepathically.

Parkinson was Irene's Spirit control. He had been working through her during her many years of transfiguration and we lovingly referred to him as the master of ceremony. As the seance was finishing, he suddenly turned his head a little to the left, and pointed to the corner of the room where François was sitting. He said: "There is a great light here and someone wishes to make his presence known to him. They were together in a past life as monks, and he wants him to know that they are waiting for him, and will be there to meet him when the time arrives." As he formed his face, I suddenly had a flashback to the night François had sat in on my course and the person who had come through for him. I asked if I could ask him a question, and he nodded. "Is your name Sebastian?" He said "Yes", and then I knew that the spirit who had come through in my class a few months before, and had called François "brother", was this same soul who had been with him in a past life. He was taking this opportunity to come through once again to encourage him.

François got through the winter and spring in his own happy way, keeping busy with all kinds of hobbies and visiting with family and friends. If he were in pain, it never showed; and I don't believe he was taking anything in the way of medication.

During the summer months, his mother went to work in a presbytery ten miles away. She would come home every night, and François would often drive up to stay with her, as he loved the peace and quiet of that little town. His younger brother was going through puberty as all teenagers do, and the friction in the family at certain times got on François' nerves; so when his mother asked if he would like to stay at the presbytery for a few days as a vacation, he jumped at the chance.

François enjoyed being there so much that he kept putting off his return home. His dad and brother would drive up to spend some time with them every few days. Time marches on and waits for no man; so it was for François! He kept himself busy with all kinds of things, and was always good natured and teasing. He was getting thinner, but always kept his faith. He knew he was going to a better world, and was looking forward to his time of transition to the World of Spirit. I would drive up to see him each week, and we would talk about all kinds of spiritual things, or whatever he felt like talking about. Norman, a friend with whom he had grown up, would come up to spend time with him as often as he could.

As September arrived, he was getting weaker and thinner; and Norman was there many hours each day. To keep busy, François had his family buy him scale models of sport cars. He and Norman would work, sometimes into the early hours of the morning, gluing the hundreds of pieces together, until they had a perfect model car.

Sunday night, the 22nd of September, Nicole called and asked if I would come up. François was deteriorating fast and wanted to see me. I planned to spend the night sitting up with him so his mother could get some sleep. Norman was there, and they had spent most of the night before working on a special Ferrari Model, which François absolutely wanted to finish before he passed on. He was very excited that he had been able to do so.

I sat in a chair in his room and we talked about many things. He wanted to know if I thought he would leave that night, because he really wanted to go while I was there with him. I answered, "You know, my love, that I have always told you that it was up to you when you would leave your body. You only have to step out of it, and you can go *anytime you wish*." He had a large statue of the Virgin Mary on his bureau, and said he didn't need anything else; she was there to help him. His mother gave him his injections of pain killer, but he didn't want to wake her up during the night; so he went through and didn't ask for it. He said that the pain was bearable, and Mother Mary was there with him. Halfway through the night, Norman came in to replace me so I could get a few hours' sleep. When morning came, he was still with us, smiling as usual. I was invited to stay for breakfast with his mother and the parish priest for whom she worked. When I went back to his room to kiss him before leaving, he made me laugh by asking if I had tried the muffins.

Around eleven the following morning, Nicole called to tell me that François had passed on a half hour before! She had been sleeping on a cot which had been set up in the office next to his downstairs room. The priest, Maurice, was sitting with him, and François had been sleeping. About 7:30 he suddenly groaned and let out a loud cry. I am certain that this was to call his mother, because he felt he was going. She rushed in, and Maurice put the statue of Mother Mary on the bed where Stephane could see it, and started to say the rosary out loud. His father and brother came to join them in the vigil, and at 10:20 he drew his last breath. When I arrived, his body was still in the room. I could sense his spirit around, but there was nothing more I could do at that time. Before going back home, I told Nicole not to bother with lunch at the house, that I would make several loaves of sandwiches and bring them over. While working at the table in my kitchen, preparing the sandwiches, François was dancing around right beside me, in his astral body, as big as life, and trying very hard to make me laugh. This was his way of telling me that he was "still alive!"

Although it poured the day of the funeral, the small country church was filled to the rafters. François had passed to spirit in the place of his choice, and wanted the service to be in the church on the same grounds. Maurice, the priest with whom François had a great affinity, and who had given him such loving care during his last months, officiated at the service. It was beautiful, and even he could not hold back the tears when he talked about the lesson in courage and love which François had given to so many. Most of the songs which François had wanted played at his funeral were sung by a wonderful choir. I knew that he had a choice place in the front row, and was certainly very pleased that everything had proceeded just as he had wanted!

Two months after his passing, Irene Griffey came back for another ten day transfiguration session. During one of the seances, Parkinson had called a number, as was his usual custom; but before he had time to say anything, he turned his head slightly to the left. Someone was breaking in with special information. Looking at me, he said that there was a young man here "who wanted to say thank you for all you did for him." Parkinson said, "It was exactly as you told him it would be; he only put one foot out, and he was there! Everyone was there to meet him, even all your guides were there to greet him. He says he wants you to know that it is as beautiful as you said it would be, and he is very happy to be there." François formed his face, and smiled at everyone, saying that he wished we could all see the beauty that was really the afterlife. I had trouble seeing his face through my tears, as for the first time, I cried for François! They were more tears of joy, although I had to admit that I missed his physical presence. This was also a healing for me, for I had never allowed myself to feel the physical emotion of his leaving. One thing I have had to learn is that even though I teach natural, spiritual and karmic law, and try to live by them as much as I can, I must keep things in perspective. We must always remember that we have to work out the emotional side of each thing in our lives, as *humanity is on the planet to evolve the emotional body*. In consultations with my clients, I describe the emotional body as a pressure cooker in which the pressure keeps building up if we don't deal with things as they come up in our lives. The tear ducts are one of the most important parts of the body, because it is through tears flowing that we get the releasing and cleansing in the emotional body. Most emotional problems are caused by a building up, sometimes for many years, of all the "garbage" we keep in the emotional body. At some point, the Universe will bring a situation into our lives to take us to the very bottom, to force the tears to flow, sometimes in spite of ourselves. *But one way or another, it will be brought back into balance.* Parkinson then went on to say that the young man was very evolved; and having been so well prepared for his transition, even though he had only been over a short period of time, had already found a group with which to work. François was busy helping young people on earth get off drugs, by influencing through the mind.

François would come in now and then to see how I was doing. I always knew when he was around, because I would feel in the area of my chest all the symptoms he had before he passed over. It would just happen suddenly, and I would know that he wanted to talk; so I would sit down, take a few deep breaths and go into my altered state, where we could be on the "same wavelength". He would never stay long; it were as if he only came in to touch base for a few moments. During that time, he was often in his home to help his family, especially his mother. Nicole would sense his presence, and feel him caressing her face. All the emotions she had held back during those two years started to come to the surface, and she went through a rough time for awhile. In the beginning, she would ask his advice about things in her life. He would answer "yes" by touching her face, and if there were nothing happening, she would know that it was "no". But after awhile, he would not decide for her; and she understood that he was telling her that she had free will, and had to make her own decisions.

Five months after he passed on, I was sitting at my living room table preparing some Spiritual work when I suddenly felt my whole chest on fire; I knew François had come in. I laughed, took a deep breath and said, "O.K. Where are you?" He was standing in one of the doorways to the living room, as big as life and as handsome as when he was here. His arm was around a young girl at his side. He was so excited, and said, "It's Carole, I've found her, I've found her!" The girl was so beautiful, very small and thin, and was dressed in a pink and white cotton dress that came above her knees. Her shoulder length hair was dark blond, parted in the middle and very straight. But what struck me the most was that she was barefoot. Somehow I immediately knew who she was! I had a flashback to a letter François had brought me a few months after his first stay in a Montreal hospital. He had become friends with a young woman who was about twenty-five, and who was also there for treatment for advanced cancer. He had told me that with the medication they had given her, she had gained about sixty pounds. When he came home, they corresponded for awhile, and then François got lax in his writing. A few months later, when he answered her last letter, he never received a reply. He brought it to me to see if I could pick up something from the vibration of her letter. On touching it, I immediately knew that she had passed to spirit, and told him so. I had forgotten the incident and had no recollection of her name, nor could I remember what had happened to the letter. I called Nicole to share the experience with her and to ask if she could remember what the girl's name had been. She couldn't remember, but her husband, Raymond, said that he thought her name was Carole. Nearly four years later, while cleaning out the cupboards in my center, I found her letter. The name was indeed Carole! When they appeared to me together that day, I remember thinking what a beautiful soul she was, and wondered what level in the Spirit World she was on, that it took François five months to find her.

During the months when I am home in Canada, I always do my share of work for several Spiritualist Churches and centers in Montreal. One Sunday I was lecturing in the First Spiritual Church about fifty miles away. I planned to talk on reincarnation and past lives. At the end of my lecture, I wanted to share the experience about François and Sebastian, and I had felt him very strongly around me as I had written my notes. The minute I sat on the podium I started to get the chest symptoms very strongly, and I knew he was there with me. I asked him telepathically to please step back so I could breathe easier, but he was influencing me so much that I had trouble getting my ideas in order. When I started to speak, I told the congregation what was happening, and laughingly said, "It seems François wants me to speak about him first, and so I shall!" This was his loving way of letting people know that he really did still exist, and to be able to share in my experience that day. Valerie Berry, a wonderful medium and close friend, was working with me that day giving clairvoyant messages, which is always part of a Spiritualist service. When Val got up, she said that she had been picking up the name François from the moment she sat down on the podium, and that she had been planning to start her messages by asking "if anyone *could take* a François." But the moment I started to talk, she knew to whom he belonged!

He surprised me with a visit one other time, which pleased me very much. It also made me realize how closely he kept in touch, and how easy it is for our loved ones in the Spirit World to reach us. A friend in Burlington, Vermont asked me to do some readings and a workshop one weekend, and she had invited me to sleep at her home. I was comfortably installed on her living room sofa, which opened up into a double bed. I was having trouble falling asleep and my mind was just wandering, but I know that I had not consciously thought of François until I suddenly felt the chest pains. I picked him up immediately, standing right beside my bed at head level. He had a big smile on his face and was in a very playful mood. He told me that he had brought Jean with him, and they were traveling all over. Jean Gauthier was a young man with whom he had grown up, and his parents, Jeannine and Bruno, have been good friends of my family for many years. Jean made his parents proud, because he worked hard in school and had never given them a moment of worry, always keeping busy at some job or another. He was a very quiet and shy boy, but knew what he wanted to do with his life, and had a bright future ahead of him. In 24 hours, this was all wiped out! When he was twenty years old he had an aneurysm in his head and died within a few hours. It was such a shock to his parents and everyone else who knew him, because here was a boy who had never touched drugs or anything harmful, and was liked by everyone. Jeannine came to see me, and finally took my courses to help her try to understand. She and his sister, Christine, came to several transfiguration sessions, and Jean never failed to come through for them. Knowing the shy, quiet personality he was, I was not surprised to see him still standing in the doorway between the kitchen and living room that night in Vermont. Not having known me like François had, he was still too shy to come any closer.

Several months after François' passing, I felt the need to let the people who had known him, and others who hadn't had the privilege, share the wisdom and knowledge of this beautiful soul. Therefore I wrote his story and sent it to one of the local papers. My deep appreciation goes to Mrs.

Gisele Lefebvre of the newspaper *L'étoile* in Dorion, Que. for printing every word, even though it took up a half page of space. I knew she was a lovely lady who came from the heart, and would understand. *This is what I wrote:*

Coteau-du-Lac

TESTIMONIAL TO FRANÇOIS SABOURIN, DECEASED ON THE 24TH OF SEPTEMBER, 1985, AT THE AGE OF 19 YEARS AND 10 MONTHS

François made his transition from our world to a better world at 10:20 a.m. on the 24th of September, 1985 and he was received with open arms by many souls who had been waiting for him for a long time, especially his good friend Jean, who had preceded him three years before, at the age of 20.

In April 1983, he learned that he had cancer. After two periods of hospitalization and a few chemotherapy treatments he made the decision to stop all treatment and to live fully the time he had left.

I had the privilege and the joy to follow the evolution of his soul during his illness.

The first time François came to see me, he was already aware of his illness. He was magnificent! I knew that I had before me a young physical body, but a soul full of wisdom. He told me that when he made his decision to stop all treatment, he felt a great sense of inner peace, and immense joy filled his heart.

He continued in these words: "My physical body is finished, and it can no longer serve me to help others as I wanted, so I have decided to go back to the other side, because I can help a lot more people from over there."

He often came to talk with me and I was able to help him to understand many things at a Spiritual level, and the new life that awaited him on the other side.

His mother, Nicole, who was the love of his life, followed him every step of the way, accepting his decisions. I have difficulty expressing my admiration for her; the courage and serenity she showed facing all the difficult times have earned her a special place in my heart forever.

Last November, François and his mother consented to share the experience they were living by participating in an hour-long television program at a Montreal station. It was a beautiful testimonial!

Following this program, each week the station received many letters and telephone calls from people who wanted to help François live his illness and transition through thoughts of love and Light, and through prayers.

I would like to share with you one of the letters François received at Christmas:

My Dear François,

What a beautiful testimonial you gave us on the television! What struck me the most about you is your calmness in facing the separation. You are young, François, you are in the prime of your life, but you are not afraid to go. Yes, you have understood that life down here is only temporary, and you have arrived at the end of your earthly voyage. Something else, much more marvelous, awaits you on the other side. You, who are a beloved child of the Eternal Father, can contemplate His Beauty... His Light which is hidden to us down here.

François, in watching you on T.V., I felt in my soul the great happiness which will be yours, and I shared that joy. I congratulate you for accepting, with your lovely smile, the will of the One who holds out his arms. Yes, go in peace my brother. I pray for you and yours, that this crossing be made in love. You have the chance to have close to you, your friend, "your mother". I bless her for helping you take the step. Her courage and strength fortify me.

François, if you can, think of me when you are in the glorious celebration. I want so much to be ready the day of the great departure. I am not young; my sixty years remind me that soon I will have to leave my physical body, but I don't have the perfect calmness I would like to feel facing these changes. A testimonial like yours gives me confidence, and I pray to have the strength to smile when my time comes.

Dear François, embrace your mother for me; I am keeping you both in my heart and in my prayers.

A friend who accompanies you in thought.

———

Thanks to François and his conception of life, many people will have more courage and perceive their physical departure from the earth plane in a different way, happy to return to the House of the Father, where our spirit lives on.

François lived the time he had left in his own way, sowing love to everyone along his pathway. He asked only three things of God:

1. To be able to make the transition in his own environment

2. Not to suffer too much

3. To be able to give a message to his mother at the end

His three desires were granted, because the spark of life was softly extinguished with all his family at his side, including his good friend Maurice, for whom he had much affection.

He was lucid and talking until two hours before the end, always with his usual sense of humor that he had kept all through his illness. His great faith in God, and especially in Mother Mary, permitted him to lift himself above the physical pain.

It was with great impatience that he awaited the *huge* party promised him when he arrived on the other side, and he always said that he hoped they would have a "black forest cake" for him.

François, Farewell My Love! Don't Forget Your Promise To Watch Over Us From Up There. You And I Know That It Is Only *"Till We Meet Again!"*

I mentioned earlier in the chapter that François' father, Raymond had suffered for several years from kidney failure, and that he had been on dialysis three times a week throughout those years. The doctors had told him from the beginning that he was unable to have a kidney transplant because of a virus in his blood. In 1988, Raymond's condition had deteriorated so badly that he was very thin and weak, his skin had a strange translucent color, and friends told me that he couldn't go on much longer. I felt really sad, and he was often in my thoughts during the months I was here in Florida. When I arrived home in the Spring, I received the wonderful news that he had been given a transplant and was doing just great! When I saw Raymond for the first time after his operation, I couldn't believe that this was the same man; his color was back to normal, and so was his weight! From what

I have heard, there has never been any problem caused by his body rejecting the new kidney. I am sure that François worked diligently from the Spirit World, to see that his dad had some good years ahead of him after all the suffering he had been through.

Last Picture of François – 1984

Chapter Thirteen

POTPOURRI OF CASES
IN ANSWER TO QUESTIONS

QUESTION # 1

−How long can a spirit stay earthbound?

As long as it takes for them to accept the Light; it can be moments after the passing, or it can be hundreds of years, if there is some particular reason why they refuse to go to the other side. I then share with them what I believe is one of my most important cases, which will probably be considered unbelievable to many who will read this. But at that moment in my work, I was living so many "unbelievable" experiences that they just became part of the normal everyday occurrence for me.

CASE # 1

One day I received a call from a woman living about twenty-five miles from my home. She had been sensing a lot of negativity in her home for a few weeks and felt something was wrong; someone told her to call me. Her husband had committed suicide in the bathroom of this house, and she thought he might be the one manifesting.

I made an appointment to see her a few days later and took Bernard with me. As we walked into the house, we sensed the negativity right away. We went to discern the bathroom first. I felt the energy of what had happened there, but I knew it was not the real problem. We walked up the stairs to the bedrooms on the second floor. On entering the first small one at the head of the stairs, we both felt something so negative that I saw it as a mass of black energy. I asked her if anyone slept in that room; because if someone did, I felt they must be very depressed from sleeping in such negative vibrations. She said that one of her daughters slept there; and yes, she was very depressed and on the verge of a nervous breakdown. I told her to move her out of there immediately! She mentioned to me that she had slept there once herself, and had awakened in the middle of the night to see a man dressed in strange clothing standing beside her bed. She screamed, and he de-materialized by slowly sinking down through the floor. The spirit was keeping a very low profile, as if he didn't want us to know that he was there. We decided to meditate on it from home and ask the guides about the problem. We blessed each room, put the Light all around the house, and told her we would be in touch with her again within a few days.

We decided to go through Mario for information. The next night I went to Maria's home where the family group of five mediums met. They told me they had been given the identity of the negative spirit in that house; it was King Herod, the one who had played such an important role in the crucifixion of Jesus! As often happens when we do this work, the spirit in the house follows us home, and tries to manifest there to scare us. Herod was no different. He was throwing things around, making noise in the bedroom and causing other phenomena to happen in Maria's house.

Because I was exhausted and needed to get away for a few days, I headed for my favorite place, the mountains in Stowe, Vermont. Basking in the energy of those magnificent mountains, and meditating beside a babbling brook, regenerated my physical, mental and emotional bodies, permitting me to get back in balance and into alignment with my soul once again.

When I returned from my short vacation and met with my family group again, they told me what had transpired while I had been gone. They said that Herod had stayed in their home, manifesting as usual, and they decided to hold a seance. Ginette would go into trance and Bernard would control. As they formed a circle around the kitchen table, Ginette's husband, Robert, sat on her left. He was a handsome young man with hair down to his shoulders, which was the style in the early eighties. I always told people that if I ever wanted to do a movie on Jesus, Robert was the one I would choose to play the part. For me, his face was exactly the way I had always pictured Jesus' would be.

They were finally able to convince Herod to control Ginette's body. As he came in, he looked to the left, trying to recognize his surroundings. When he saw Robert, he screamed and threw his arms up over his face! Even though it had been nearly two thousand years, I am sure he had never forgotten what had happened. Otherwise he would not have been afraid to cross to the other side. Bernard started to talk to him, trying to convince him to leave; but he became very angry and said he wasn't going anywhere! He insisted that he was a king and was still in charge of his Kingdom, and no one could remove him from his throne. They argued with him, explaining that he was no longer a king and had to leave and go to the Light! After awhile, they finally got through to him. He agreed to leave, but was not happy about it. Afterwards other spirits came through; family members who came in for a short chat, or the odd soul rescue case, and finally a guide came to talk to them. He told them that the Spirit World had sent Herod back down, and that they would have to put him over another time. The guide explained that when Herod went over, Jesus had to be the one to receive him. He was away that night and therefore not available for this task. They waited a few days and tried again; this time it was all right. The guide told them later that Jesus had taken Herod in his arms and said: "Herod, as long a time as you have been lost and wandering, this length of time shall you be with me in my Kingdom!" Needless to say, everyone was crying when that seance was over!

A few days later, I called Maria and she told me that Herod was back and up to his usual antics! I asked her why he had come back, and she told me that the guides said that I had talked about the case, and this had drawn him right back down. When you are involved in something as awesome as this, it is difficult not to share it with your children or best friend, especially since I had not been advised by the guides that to do so would draw them back into the earth's atmosphere. They told her that when we did a case, we were not to listen to the tape or talk about it for a couple of weeks. This gives the spirit time to get used to its new home, and to acquire the spiritual awareness needed to accept that it must stay in that dimension. As she was telling me this, I felt a heaviness at the back of my head which, to me, means a negative entity or energy. Suddenly the putrid smell of a backed up toilet came in. I knew that Herod was manifesting this odor for my benefit to try to scare me. Bursting into laughter, I told Maria to tell him I preferred the smell of roses! As I said this, I instantly felt him standing behind my chair. He had just projected himself into my center, and I told Maria that I would call her back.

I turned my chair facing the one my clients always sat in when they came for a reading, and sternly said: "Herod, sit down, I want to talk to you!" He sat down immediately and I could see him clearly with my physical eyes as well as clairvoyantly. He was dressed in a long white robe with a braided gold sash with beautiful tassels tied around his waist. I knew that he had been a tall man, for his head was above the back of the chair, which was quite high. He had rather narrow shoulders and a slim body. As I took a moment to examine him, I was shocked to realize that tears were flowing down his face! I dialed Maria and asked her to confirm with the guides that this was actually happening. They said: "Yes, he is crying! He is asking Carole's forgiveness for all the trouble he has caused!" I hung up the phone and turned towards him with tears in my own eyes, for I felt so much sorrow for this soul who had wandered in darkness for nearly two thousand years. Understanding karma the way I do, I knew that he had played a part in a scenario that was to happen at that point in the history of mankind. When we realize, that the coming of Christ and his crucifixion was prophesied hundreds of years before it happened, some people had to play a key role in order for the prophesy to come to pass. I saw this lost soul as one of these.

I turned back to him, held out my hands, and gently asked him to put his hands in mine, which he did. I spoke to him lovingly, and told him it was time for him to go to his new life on the other side. His time on earth was finished for awhile, and there would be a much better existence for him over there. His energy changed completely. He thanked me for my help, and he was gone!

QUESTION # 2

– CAN NEGATIVE ENTITIES POSSESS OR INJURE A MEDIUM WHO DOES THIS WORK?

Most mediums refuse to do soul rescue work if at all possible. As mediums begin to develop, their auras change and they become beacons of Light to lost souls. If they don't have a reliable person in the physical who knows how to control, there could be problems.

CASE # 2

Although she had never taken any courses, Johanne had wonderful mediumship potential. She was friendly with Linda, a woman who had taken my beginners and advanced classes when I first started in the early eighties. Linda has gone on to develop her potential as a healer, and is doing excellent work in the field. They decided to sit together a few nights a week to meditate. Johanne, being very open to spirit but never having learned how to protect herself, realized that lost souls started taking over her body without her consent. Linda did not know how to handle the problem; she did not realize that once a spirit has controlled a human body, someone has to convince it to leave. Besides, she did not want the spirit released in her house. The fact that Johanne was a very sensitive and emotional person served only to help this spirit manifest stronger. Johanne was in a bad way, feeling the pain and the emotions of this spirit as if they were her own. She started to panic and begged for help. A third person sitting with them decided that something had to be done and, after a long period of time, was able to convince it to leave.

CASE # 3

In 1985 Therese called asking if I would visit a house belonging to some people she knew who were having some problems. We set the date. I had promised Maria, a good friend of mine, that I would take her with me. She wanted to learn more about doing soul rescue, because she often had lost souls, who had committed suicide, contact her in her home; and she didn't know what to do with them. I thought this would be a good chance for her to have a few lessons, and maybe we could do some work together. She was a born medium, and could see spirits from the time she was a small child; in fact, they were her playmates during all of her childhood years.

At the last minute I was unable to go due to an illness. Not wanting to disappoint them, Therese decided to go as planned.

Not really having learned how to handle these cases, Maria walked into the house with her chakras and aura wide open. Another friend, Edie, had come along to help, but she didn't have much experience in this work either. They started to discern, and went down to the basement where they felt the negativity strongly. They then entered the garage which was adjacent to the basement. As soon as they walked in, a very negative spirit controlled Maria and threw her to the cement floor! He yanked off her jewelry and threw it violently to one side. Still on his hands and knees, he tried to grab Edie. He was screaming and yelling, and using vulgar language! At some point he roughly put his hand under Maria's dress (remember he was in her body). The family had accepted that a few friends assist, and of course their panic at what was happening provided him with the energy needed to manifest so strongly. Therese was finally able to convince him to go to the Light, with promises of all kinds, including women waiting for him, booze, etc. He told them his name was Ismael, and he was a black man who had escaped from Africa in 1895. When he left Maria's body, an even more violent spirit took over immediately. They decided to quit, and wait for me to finish the task a couple of days later. They got the second one out of Maria, but he immediately possessed the dog, who started to run around in circles, barking and biting his masters, and urinating all over the floors.

The next day, along with all the black and blue marks on her arms and legs, Maria realized she also had marks in the pubic and vagina area.

On Monday night we went back together. Since the grandparents were having problems as well, we decided to start at their house next door. I showed Maria how to completely close herself off before going in, as I always keep my medium's aura closed until I have discerned each room, and decided where I wanted them to sit for the exorcism. Once we are all prepared, with the Crucifix, Holy Water, candles and incense in place, I let them go into trance. I am ready for anything, as I never really know what to expect; although I have a good idea from the vibrations in the house, whether it is negative or not.

While discerning in the basement, we psychically saw an elderly woman in a corner of the room; I knew she had to go. Maria had also picked up her vibration, feeling that she had come into that house because she was attached to an old antique clock which she had once owned. On questioning the owners afterward, they showed us a very old clock which they had bought at a flea market many years before, and which they kept in the den in the basement.

We prepared everything in the living room, and Maria sat down in a large chair. She was immediately entranced by the spirit of the old lady, who came in manifesting strongly; her name was Lisette de la Croix. She said that this was **HER** house and the other lady (the owner) kept moving the furniture around! I told her that the house was not hers, that she had died, and now had to go on. She refused to believe that she was dead, and I asked her what year it was. She said that it was 1905, and I answered that it was now 1985. It was impossible that she would still be living in the physical. She started to cry and said that she couldn't be dead because she would have to burn in Hell! I told her that Hell didn't exist, and she said, "Yes it does, because the bishop told me I would burn in Hell!" She kept arguing and pleading that I not make her leave, but I finally convinced her. She grabbed my hands, which were on her lap. She held on to them so hard that her nails left marks on my hands. She made me swear that she wouldn't burn in Hell, which I did with much love. Suddenly she looked in front of her, and her eyes widened with shock as she recognized her mother, who had come to get her. She screamed, "Mama!", held out her arms, and immediately left the body!

It made me sad and angry to think of the millions of souls who were still earthbound, or living in darkness, because their religion taught them that God was not a God of love, but one who judged and punished. Therefore they expected and feared this! This kept them from advancing on their soul paths in the Divine Light, which is our Spiritual heritage.

QUESTION # 3

− DOES PSYCHIC ATTACK REALLY EXIST?

The human psyche is so delicate that it is not something we play around with! This is why it is so important to me that all of my students begin with the basic course for several weeks, and learn how to protect themselves first and foremost. Psychic attack really exists; and as the negativity gets stronger and stronger on the planet, we all become more vulnerable!

When we do this work, we need to keep our shield of protection around us at all times, only opening up when there is a need. Sometimes I would like to be more open and tuned in to the psychic, as some people are, but I know that this is not for me. I decide when I want to tune in to someone or something, keeping my "feelers" out for those in need. When I sense something, I will often project healing energy to them without their even realizing it. I will only send them *white* Light, from which their bodies will take whatever color vibration it needs for the healing; we must have permission from them or someone close to them to do a real healing. This is not to say that I don't have lost souls come to me when I am working in the kitchen or elsewhere in my home. At these moments, I am grounded and doing "down to earth" things, which opens my heart chakra more. They will try to reach us wherever they can; I just send them love, ask them to go to the Light that I visualize for them, and they are on their way!

CASE # 4

Unknowingly I let my guard down while working on one of my cases back in 1982. This gave me a lesson I will never forget! I received a call from a young couple living together in an old house they had bought. The girl told me that many strange things were happening, and they sensed a presence in their home that did not belong there. The boyfriend's personality completely changed for no apparent reason, which was the cause of much friction between them. They started to argue more and more, often ending with him slamming the door on his way out, only to come back hours later not understanding why it had happened. One time when this occurred, as she stood in the middle of the kitchen crying, she felt someone take her in his arms to console her. Knowing she was alone in the house, she became frightened; and, as she looked towards the stairs to the second floor, she saw a man walking up there.

They had never had any problems with each other before moving into the house. She talked to a friend about the situation, and her friend suggested she call me. A few days later I took Bernard and Mario with me, and we discerned to see what we could find. I interviewed the young woman and she told me that over the past few weeks, whenever her boyfriend made love to her, she absolutely **knew** that it was not him performing the act, but a completely different personality!

We decided to try to bring him through Bernard. Because we felt that this was where he spent most of his time, and where the energy was the strongest, we set up a chair in the empty room next to their bedroom. I tried to coax him to come in, but he absolutely refused to control Bernard's body. We felt that he was very aggressive. Next we asked Mario to get out his paper and pencil, and try to bring him through that way. But after a few seconds, Mario's hand began to shake badly. He felt that the spirit was so angry that he was preparing to snap the pencil in two, so we stopped at once! We decided we would meditate on it, and ask the guides who it was, and the best way to get rid of him. When Mario asked through automatic writing, the guide scolded us for going there; but because we had started it, they would help us finish the task.

My weekly class was a few nights later, and he was the first spirit to control Ginette. He came through in a very angry state and warned us that he didn't want to see us there again; the girl belonged to him and he was working on getting rid of her boyfriend. She would be his forever. Because I had a large class, I had no intention of provoking a negative experience for my students who had never seen anything like this, so I just nonchalantly agreed with him. By not giving him any energy to manifest stronger, he just repeated, "Don't you come back, or you'll be sorry!", and he left.

Over the next few days I sensed that a negative entity was visiting me now and then. A foul odor would suddenly appear in my home, for which there was no explanation. One day I left the house and drove to our cottage ten miles away. On walking in the door, there was the same smell of sewers backing up; I knew that I had company! I turned on the television and laid down in a long chair to relax. I felt him come into the room, and I crossed my arms and legs to close myself off and block the energy. Suddenly the T.V. switched off by itself, and I could psychically see him standing right beside it. I laughed and said loudly, "You son of a gun! You turned it off, now you just turn it right back on and get out of here!" By lying there calmly, smiling because I was enjoying the situation, I gave him no energy to manifest further; so he turned the television back on, and left!

It was a few nights later that I woke up and had a choking sensation. I knew that I was in a long black box turned upside down, which covered me from head to foot. I could psychically see and feel that the little spark of life which we all have in the solar plexus area was slowly being extinguished! I immediately tried to call in the Light for help; but I could see nothing but darkness, and the spark was getting dimmer. I screamed at my husband who was sleeping in the bed beside me, and he sat up immediately! I said: "I know you don't know what I'm talking about, but for God's sake visualize white Light around me, quick!" He sat there for a few moments doing his best to comply, and I slowly felt the darkness around me dissipating and the black box began to disappear. The little spark of life started to flicker stronger and become brighter, and I vowed that I would never allow myself to be put in such a vulnerable position again; somehow I would learn to protect myself with Divine Light so well that nothing could ever touch me. During a reading shortly after, two male spirits, Lenny and Frank, said that from then on they would be protecting me during the sleep state, so that nothing negative could come close to me! I now understood why the guides would have preferred that we not touch this case, but I knew we would finish it somehow. To have been able to find the energy to do what he did to me, this entity had to have found help from very negative beings. But I wasn't worried, because I knew that I had God on my side, and some powerful guides working with me. A few days later, Bernard said we should go back and finish up this case. Of course I agreed.

Monday night was class night and twelve students were present. We started the meditation and Ginette was the first to go into her trance state. I recognized the entity the moment he came through; and, as he turned and looked at me, he said very angrily: "You're talking about coming back there again, and I warned you not to!"

Once again I was amazed at how spirits had knowledge of what we were saying and thinking. I answered with some anger of my own, telling him he was to leave that house immediately. He had no right to be there; he was dead and had to remain on the other side. Because he was now in another dimension, he was not allowed to bother people who were still living on the earth plane! He answered that there was no way he was leaving; he was going to convince her to come over and join him so they could be together! I told him to get out of Ginette's body immediately and go into the Light in the middle of the circle, and I silently asked the guides' help in removing him.

Jocelyne was sitting across from Ginette and was in an altered state of consciousness. As he came out and into the middle of the circle, she asked if it were possible that he could be swearing like crazy. I laughed and said it was very possible, because I could sense his anger and violence. She suddenly said, "He's trying to control me and I'm afraid!" I calmed her down and moved behind her, asking her to let him in; I would work with him from there. But as he approached he sensed what had happened to her a few years before, when black magic had been used against her over a long period of time. Much damage had been done to her physical and etheric body, and it is through the grace of God that she is still on the earth plane today. She still has physical problems because of the terrible things that were done to her through jealousy. Because of his own negativity, or perhaps the guides projected it to him, he was able to feel the damage that had been caused to her by evil people. He started to complain, "Whew! She's worse than I am. I sure don't want to stay in her, I'm getting out of here!" I said, "Yes, get into that Light and don't come back. You stay away from that young woman. She doesn't belong to you and never will, because you're dead and she is still living on the earth plane!" I saw him go into the Light and the vibrations in the room changed.

This confirmed for me the torture Jocelyne had been through! Shortly after she came to me for the first time looking for help, having exhausted all other avenues, she started my classes to learn to protect herself from psychic attack and to develop her mediumship and healing gifts.

The house quieted down after we terminated the work, and I never heard from them again. A few years later, someone who knew them told me that they had separated; but there was no other information she could give me.

CASE # 5

A few weeks after Jocelyne started with me, a guide asked me to help them do an exorcism on her, because the people involved in the black magic were still trying to harm her. They didn't want it to be done during a class, but asked that I choose only one of my students to assist me. I chose one who liked to accompany me when I did soul rescue cases, and we prepared to do the exorcism a few nights later. It took about three hours and was quite difficult! The woman who instigated the black magic spells against Jocelyne was aware of what was happening through information received from the negative entities on the lower astral plane.

At some point, she projected herself into the room and controlled Jocelyne's physical body. The guide channeling at that moment warned us, and left me to handle the situation. She was a very vindictive person and said that she wanted to possess Jocelyne because she loved her; if she couldn't have her, no one else would! I sensed some lesbian tendencies in her personality and had to get verbally rough and finally forced her to leave. It took nearly three hours, as the guide had me do healing on the different parts of Jocelyne's body that had been damaged.

Jocelyne's experiences were unbelievable. It was only her faith that God would put someone on her pathway who could help her, and her love for her young son, that kept her going through those traumatic and painful years. I taped everything and believe there is enough material for another book on Jocelyne's story. I know that at some point in her life, these evil people literally "put her to death", and she went to the other side. She made a covenant with God that if He would allow her to return and raise her little son, she would dedicate her life to His work, in one way or another. Besides being one of the best mediums I developed, she was a wonderful healer, and I am sure she is using her energy in some capacity to advance God's work on this planet.

Several weeks before I did the exorcism, I was at a seance with the family group. Ginette was in trance, and a spirit came through holding something in her hand. Ginette turned to me and the Spirit said she was St. Theresa; she had been sent by God to bring a Blessing for protection. She told me that there was a group of dangerous people who had found out where I lived, and they were working against me with the help of beings from the dark side of life! They were bombarding me and my center with the black light, because I was helping a young woman with a bad problem. But she said that Divine Light was so strong around my center that their black light would just bounce off and go back to them, and they would be destroyed. She handed me a beautiful rose that I could see clairvoyantly, which she said was for the wonderful work I was doing. Even after all these years, I have never forgotten her beautiful vibration and loving voice. I knew that Jocelyne was the person to whom St. Theresa was referring.

QUESTION # 4

– HOW ARE SOULS DIRECTED FOR HELP?

Over the years, souls have come in for help in some of the most unusual ways!

CASE # 6

A few years ago, I received a phone call from Rene, the secretary at the Montreal S.S.F. Center where I am an active member, working at the services during the months I am home in Canada. He said that a student from a Montreal university wanted to interview a Spiritualist Minister for a paper she was doing on how different religions perceive death; and would I meet with her? I immediately accepted, and told him I would be in the City on Thursday.

Sylvia was waiting for me when I arrived, and we went to the library because it was nice and quiet. She took out her tape recorder and her list of questions, and we started working. We must have been about a half hour into the interview when suddenly, very close to me on the right, a spirit appeared. He was very thin and sitting in a wheelchair, with his head slumped to his chest. I sensed that he was very depressed, and had not gone to the Light as he should have. I felt he had died in his fifties, and from the symptoms I was feeling in my own body, I knew he had died of cancer. I could see him sitting in his wheelchair in a hospital room, in the same state of depression. He was looking out the window, feeling very lonely, but not wanting anyone to visit because of his deteriorating body. I felt that he probably didn't even want his family to see him this way! I asked Sylvia if she recognized him, because he came in on her vibration, and belonged to her or someone around her. She said that all the details I was giving matched those of her sister-in-law's father, who had died a few years before.

I knew someone from the other side had brought him in for me to help, so I visualized the Light in front of him. Assuring him that there would be someone there to help him, I asked him to go into the Light. Sylvia said that her sister-in-law Polly would be very happy to hear what had happened, and would certainly be in touch with me!

About a year later I received a call from a young woman identifying herself as Polly, Sylvia's sister-in-law. She asked for an appointment with me, and I gave it to her at 4:00 p.m. a few days later. As usual, I was busy working in the office that day. At 3:00 o'clock I suddenly felt sick from head to toe, as if I were having an "instant virus" or something! My head was aching and my whole vibration was out of kilter. I thought, "My God, what's happening here? I've got a reading to do in an hour, and there's no way I can do it in this condition!" Polly had already left her home, for it would take her an hour to drive to my town from Montreal; and there was no way I could reach her to cancel the appointment. All of a sudden I felt a presence near me and started to laugh! I always marvel at how the spirits know what is happening around us. Here was Polly's dad, an hour early for the rendezvous, as if he wanted to be certain he wouldn't miss it! I lovingly asked him to step back out of my aura, because I was feeling in my own body, all the symptoms he had had before he died. I told him to be patient, that Polly would be here in a short while, and he could be with us. As he moved back, everything returned to normal, and I went on with my typing. When Polly arrived, I told her that her dad had arrived before she did, because he didn't need to take a taxi!

When I started, his presence was very strong in the room. I gently asked him to wait until I had finished the reading, and then he could talk to Polly. I felt a very loving vibration and he was very patient. As we finished, he stepped up beside her, and there was a woman with him. He was standing with his arm around her waist, and I felt a strong love connection between the two of them. Suddenly I knew who she was, and said: "Polly, your mom is also in the Spirit World, isn't she?" She answered "Yes"! I didn't channel him, as I sometimes do during my readings, but was picking up everything he was saying through clairvoyance. I relayed this information to Polly. Her father wanted her to know that he and her mom had talked everything out in the Spirit World. They now understood each other and were together. (I felt that there were many years of drinking problems, which Polly confirmed.) He suddenly projected the color blue, which to me means healing. I knew he was trying to let Polly know that they were helping with a situation around her on the earth plane, where someone needed healing. He showed me a young man who was pacing up and down a room, over and over. It reminded me of a caged lion, and I felt a great deal of mental and emotional confusion in this person. Polly said her brother had been out of work for some time, and was trying hard to find a job. He wasn't sleeping at night, pacing up and down his room a lot, and at times seemed very depressed! Her dad confirmed that this was about whom he was talking, and told her to give him moral support and love. He gave me a few more messages for her, and said he regretted some of the things he had done while on earth, but nothing could be changed now. He wanted her to understand that the problem he had had was like a sickness. He stayed until the end of the reading, and left her with a feeling of much love to remember him by.

CASE # 7

In August 1990, I was working at a week long symposium of our S.S.F. Chapter in Minnesota. The mediums and clairvoyants worked during the lunch and dinner hour, at which time the participants had finished their workshops, and could book appointments with the reader of their choice. We started at 12:00 p.m., and, while waiting for my first client, I decided to rest for fifteen minutes. As I lay on my bed, I suddenly felt a sharp pain in my chest and had difficulty breathing. The pain going down my left arm signified to me that the person also suffered from angina. I often get information clairvoyantly before my clients arrive, and the first thought I had was that my 12:00 o'clock appointment was an elderly man who suffered from a heart problem. I was curious to see if I were right. I looked at my list and my first reading was for a man.

When he walked in, I was surprised to find that he was a young man, about thirty years of age, whose name was Chris. I didn't feel that the symptoms belonged to him; but as we sat facing each other, a spirit immediately made his presence known by stepping up beside him. I could see an elderly man and felt that he was his grandfather. I described him to Chris, and he acknowledged that his grandfather had passed to spirit through a heart attack about ten years before. He could sense his presence very close to him as he sat there. I asked the spirit to step back so I could do the reading, and then we would be able to speak to him; but he felt he had waited long enough, and refused to wait another minute. He stepped in between us and blocked my energy, so that I could not tune into his grandson to do the reading. I explained to Chris that we would have to do a soul rescue as his grandfather was quite confused, and I felt that he had never really gone to the Light. I channeled him through me, and he was very emotional about finally being able to get in touch with someone from his family. He had had a heart attack, and the sudden death had been a great shock to him. That would explain why he hadn't gone on. Chris talked to him lovingly, and told him how much the family all loved and missed him. After consoling his grandfather, Chris convinced him that he now had to leave and go to the Light. I said that he had been a very strong personality while in the physical, and never took no for an answer! Chris smiled and said: "That was my grandpa!"

Wherever I go, something always seems to happen; and I end up doing soul rescue in one way or another! In February, 1991, I was booked for two weeks of spiritual work back in Canada for the S.S.F. Centers in Saskatoon, Saskatchewan, and Winnipeg, Manitoba. I flew first to Saskatoon for an intensive ten days of lectures, workshops and consultations. On my first day there, Phyllis and Gerry, who are in charge of the center, had booked me for an interview with two different television stations. While waiting for my turn at the second station, we watched the monitor as a young man and woman were being interviewed. They were both comedians who were appearing for the week at the hotel where I was staying. They had heard the subject of my interview, and wanted to stay and watch. When I was through, we started chatting. Tim shared an experience that happened when he was young, which made him a believer, and he wanted me to confirm that it was possible. Tim explained that when he was a teenager, he and two friends were fooling around. One of them, on a dare or whatever, decided to climb what looked like a telephone pole! As he got to the top, he accidentally brushed against a wire and came crashing to the ground. He immediately sprang to his feet and said loudly: "Well! I guess I'll never try that again!" The next instant he fell over, and was dead! When the boys explained what had happened, the doctor said that there was no way he could have stood up; he had died the moment he touched the high tension wire! I explained to Tim that it was such a shock to him, that he had stood up in his astral body; Tim had been able to see this, as some people can.

In talking with the manager of the club where Tim was appearing, he mentioned that they had a couple of ghosts in the hotel, and many people had seen or sensed them over the years. He asked if we would be interested in helping him "get rid" of them, in exchange for dinner and a front row seat at Tim's comedy show. We readily accepted. On arriving back at the hotel, we arranged to meet a few hours later to see what was happening.

CASE # 8

The people who managed the hotel had known for years that there was a spirit in the downstairs club, as many clients had complained about sensing and seeing it. We began with that one. Phyllis and I went down to discern, and as we started walking around, we picked it up immediately near a table at the back of the room. The hair stood up on both of our necks and arms at the same time, which is always an indication of the presence of spirit for anyone who has mediumship potential. We decided to sit down at the table, and I would channel him through. He came in immediately, and I knew it was a man in his fifties who had been there for a long time. He was upset at seeing Phyllis, and asked, "What is *she* doing here? Women aren't allowed in this place!" We immediately switched to have Gerry question him, as we knew he would accept a man. It was an easy case, for he seemed bored with his life of hanging around the bar; so when Gerry asked him if he would rather try some place new for a change, he was easy to convince. Gerry visualized the Light in front of him, and asked him to go into it, and he left immediately. He went back to the time before women were allowed in bars, so he must have been there for many years.

CASE # 9

Afterwards we went to the fifth floor, where many people had sensed a presence, mostly in the hall. We walked towards the end of the hall, and felt it immediately. It was really strong! Phyllis had worked at that hotel a few years before, and had heard the story of one of the maids who, after having had an argument with her supervisor, had gone home and hung herself! When she left that day, she had threatened to do it, and told them she would haunt them for the rest of their lives!

I didn't want to put a chair in the hall where we sensed her presence, because if a client came strolling down the hall to his room, he might find our actions rather strange! Tim was staying on that floor, and we decided to use his room; I mentally asked the spirit to follow us. As soon as I sat down, she controlled me immediately. The soul was very emotional, and put her hands up to her throat and complained that she was choking! I made the motions of removing the rope from around her neck, and told her it was alright now, she could breathe easier. She had a foreign accent, and was sobbing and very angry. (Phyllis told me later that the supervisor was from a foreign country, and had imported several girls from there to work at the hotel.) She was crying and gesticulating strongly, and said loudly: "She say I not clean! Not true; I clean, I clean! Why she say I not clean? I work good, why she say I not do clean work?" Phyllis talked to her gently, but she was just too upset to listen to reason. She kept arguing that the work was done properly and **she** had no right to treat her the way she did! In my light trance state, I was conscious of everything that was happening around me, and suddenly there appeared a beautiful lady dressed in a long white gown. She had come to receive the spirit when she was ready to leave. Knowing how religious the people from her country were, and their devotion to certain Saints, I told Phyllis to tell her to look to her left; there was someone who had come to get her. She turned her head, and her face lit up with joy as she recognized her Spiritual visitor! She held out her arms and left with her.

CASE # 10

After finishing my work in Saskatoon, I flew to Winnipeg for my five days of bookings in that city. Sara, who was in charge of the Winnipeg Spiritual Center, picked me up at the airport and drove me to my hotel. I was exhausted after the ten days of intensive work, so I decided to unpack quickly and rest. I wasn't sure which bed I wanted to sleep in, so I tried the one near the window, but woke up after a short time feeling very strange! I had a bad pain running down my left arm, as well as a sharp chest pain. Because I was lying on my stomach, my solar plexus was vibrating strongly; I was feeling very emotional, and out of kilter. As I lay there tuning in to what was happening, I sensed that a man had died of a heart attack in that bed, and not realizing that he had made the transition, was still there. I was having trouble releasing the pain from my own body, and was getting ready to sit down to have a talk with him telepathically when Sara called me. I mentioned it to her, and she said she would be over shortly and we would do a soul rescue.

When Sara arrived, she sensed him immediately. I sat down, and she pulled a chair up in front of me, ready to control. He came through very emotionally as so many do, and asked: "What the hell happened? Where's my wife? Where are my children?" Sara just told him that he was dead and had to go to the Light. She kept repeating the same thing over and over, not answering his questions. (Sara does not work the same way as I do when I work with a trance medium and am the one controlling. I try to answer their questions one way or another, to give them some satisfaction; otherwise it doesn't work.) Finally I saw a woman in Spirit standing in front of me, and somehow I knew that she was his sister, Pat. I gave this information to Sara, and she said: "Your sister Pat has come to get you, and you must leave with her. Do you see her?" He acknowledged that he did, and agreed to go with her, but I could see that he was far from convinced about anything!

I awoke during the night with all the pains again, even though I was sleeping in the other bed. He had come back for his answers! I was finally able to release the pain and go back to sleep, for I was very tired, and didn't feel like getting up and dealing with the problem at that moment. The next morning I could sense him very strongly. Although I tried very hard, I was having problems releasing all the symptoms I felt. I sensed he had been earthbound for several years, and his vibrations were very strong in that hotel room. I had several readings to do in my room that day and, as I have to put myself in an altered state of consciousness, I open myself up to sensing strong abnormal vibrations around me, especially pain. This was hindering me in my consultations. When I went for lunch, I asked the manager if anyone had ever died in the hotel? He said that a woman had once died there, and he asked why I wanted to know. I explained as much as I thought he might understand, and he sort of smiled. He had taken psychology in college, and was more into that line of thinking, but stayed open to a certain degree on the rest. He asked if I wanted to change rooms and, because I had several more readings to do, I felt there was no need to suffer. It would take several days of "smudging the room" (burning sage as the north American Indians do, to remove negativity) before the vibrations could be completely cleared. He told me to move into the room across the hall, and I immediately did so. The next day the room had been assigned to two women, and I noticed them go in and out, marveling at the fact that they probably didn't feel a thing!

QUESTION # 5

– WHAT SHOULD PEOPLE DO IF THEY HAVE A GHOST IN THEIR HOME? SHOULD THEY LEAVE IT THERE?

It depends on what phenomena is happening around us, and if we feel comfortable with it. Sometimes what we perceive as a ghost could be a Guardian Angel, or a Spirit protector, whose task has been to protect us since birth, especially in the case of a person with Spiritual gifts who has an important destiny path which will only start to manifest later in life.

CASE # 11

One night in a restaurant about twenty miles from my home, I heard a lady talking about her haunted house. After my meal, I went over and introduced myself, asking if she would share with me, what I had overheard her mentioning to her friend. She was happy to do so, and said that the ghost was a small eight year old North American Indian boy. Her house was built on an old Indian burial ground, and she felt that he had probably been buried there. He had been part of the family for years, and had always been there while the children were growing up. She was very happy to have him, for he was better than any watchdog she could get for her children. Over the years, whenever one of them got involved in a dangerous situation, he always ran to warn her. Whenever the family got into the car to go somewhere, before they had a chance to start, the back door would suddenly open and close. They would always laugh, for they knew that their little protector had jumped in the back seat with the kids, intending to go along for the ride! She said that there was no way she would ever do anything to make him leave, as he was part of the family!

CASE # 12

My friend Mary had a similar experience a few years ago, before moving from the north to Florida with her six children. One morning in the early 80's she woke to find her twenty-one year old son, Don, sitting outside her bedroom door! When she asked what was wrong, he explained that during the night he was awakened by someone gently slapping his cheek. When he looked up, there was a man dressed in old fashioned clothing at the foot of his bed, holding a lantern and staring at him. Of course, he became alarmed, and ran downstairs to his mother's room! This was their first encounter with the ghost whom they came to call

"Quasimoto". The rooms upstairs were gabled, and he could only stand up in the center. That was the only time he was ever seen clearly, but they saw his shape in shadow several times. Of all the children, he seemed to be the most attached to Don. One morning, Don woke his mother to say he was late for work and wanted to know why she hadn't awakened him. They then discovered that all three clocks, which had alarms set to ring for work and school, had been disconnected; one had the alarm turned off and the two others had been disconnected at the wall socket. As they were rushing to get Don's lunch ready, they listened to the morning news. They heard that a tanker truck had crashed into some cars and exploded, at the exact moment Don would have been on the bridge which he crossed every morning to go to his job. There had been some people killed, and they felt that Quasimoto had shut off the alarms in order to save Don's life! I asked Mary if he had followed Don to Florida, for many ghosts are attached to a house rather than a person. She said he had only sensed his presence a few times in the years he had been here, and I felt that he belonged to the house in the north. He only came to say hello to his young friend once in awhile.

QUESTION # 6

–DO I, OR HAVE I EVER WORKED WITH THE POLICE?

The eyes being the mirror of the soul, I sometimes get clairvoyance where certain cases are concerned by looking at the victim's eyes in pictures in the newspaper. This seems to trigger something in me, and images start to appear spontaneously, but most of the time I block them off. When I studied at the Arthur Findlay College in England in 1983, a medium told us about a case of an eight year old girl who had been abducted in that country. It had been many months, and they had never found a trace of her. She explained that the best mediums in the country had been working on the case, and not one was able to come up with anything concrete. That was when they all backed off, because they understood that, for some karmic reason, she was not to be found immediately! There is a reason for every thing that happens, and cause and effect is involved in one way or another.

CASE # 13

About six years ago, I received a call from a woman asking if I would speak to a friend of hers who was at her house and needed some help. She passed the phone to her friend and she told me this story. She lived just across the border in the Province of Ontario about ten miles from where I lived at that time. Her neighbors were a couple in their fifties, who were living on a small farm. One day they discovered the couple had disappeared without a trace! The lady had not shown up at her place of employment for about a week. Some of the animals had died of hunger and thirst, and they thought it must have happened about ten days before. She wanted to know if I could get any information on them, and I told her it would be easier for me if I had an article that had belonged to them, either a photo or something they had touched, which would have their vibrations on it. She told me that the police were guarding the place, but that she would get me something!

When the phone rang, I had been in a state of altered consciousness, doing some work with my Spirit Doctor; and I was very relaxed. As I hung up the phone I suddenly felt a spirit come in. It was in a confused state and, when I tuned in to it, I knew immediately that it was the man about whom we had just been speaking. I saw his wife with him, and knew they were both in the Spirit World. I sensed they had been murdered, and he started projecting images to me of a young man who looked to be about thirty years old. He was very thin, and had dark straight, shoulder length hair which was parted in the middle. He was dressed in dirty jeans and a blue wool navy jacket, and I could see him very clearly. From his vibration I immediately knew that he was very often on drugs. I was surprised to have this happen so spontaneously, and I called this woman back to see if her friend was still there. After putting her on the phone, I explained what had happened and started giving her the description. When I reached the part about his being around thirty, I felt her go into shock. She asked me if he could be thirty-four, and I laughed and said, "Well I'm seeing him in my mind, so of course he could be". She explained that I had just given her the description of this couple's son and wanted to know if it were possible. Picking up my pendulum that I had just been using in my diagnosis work with Dr. Bach, I asked Spirit. They confirmed that it was definitely their son!

She returned home and told the police officer that she had contacted a medium, and I had said that their son had murdered them. I found out later that they immediately started looking for him! They picked him up a few days later in the United States, I think it was somewhere in the midwest. The police had put out an A.P.B on him, and he was stopped for a traffic violation. He was driving his dad's brand new pickup truck, which had disappeared at the same time they had.

I read in the newspaper that he had been caught and admitted killing them both, burning the bodies, and scattering the ashes all over the yard. At his trial the judge asked him why he did it, and he simply said, "Because I felt like it!" He was sentenced to life in prison, and I hope that they keep him there for the rest of his life! The police had asked her who I was, and she refused to tell them, saying that she thought I would prefer that my identity not be revealed. They said I had been responsible for their catching him so fast. They had never suspected him, and were off on a completely different trail.

These things happen spontaneously to me; I don't go looking for them. I know that homicide departments are working more and more with psychics. In fact, when I took my mediumship course with the Arthur Ford Academy, I remember Pat Hayes mentioning that a police department in a northern city had sent three or four of their detectives, who were very intuitive, to take their course. They would no longer have to use outside psychics. As much as I know that I am usually right, I have to work with someone who is open. I need to be in complete harmony with their vibrations; then I know it can be 100% correct. But the minute there is negativity or doubt on their part, I begin to doubt myself. This causes a blockage in me, and it doesn't work, as in the following case.

CASE # 14

About three years ago a young woman disappeared in Florida. As I looked at her picture, I started getting images of what happened to her as she left her apartment; but I immediately blocked it off, thinking, "What if I'm wrong?" One night I was meditating with a friend in my apartment, and I was channeling. Suddenly a soul came close to me and I was certain it was she. I heard two words, which were the name of some food. I was surprised, but remembering my days at the beginning of my work when the spirits always gave us "trivia", I knew that she was possibly giving me something to identify her. She then went on to give me more information as to what had happened to her. I told my friend that if she wanted us to do something about what we had received, her share of the work was to call the 800 number and submit the two words to her family. If they recognized this as being one of her favorite foods, I would follow through with the rest! She kept putting it off with one excuse or another. My friend moved out of Florida a few months later, and I went home to Canada for six months. I heard recently that the 800 number is still in existence, and the family continues to wait for information. Maybe one of these days I will find the right person with whom I can work, and to whom I can give the details of the cases I receive, and not worry so much whether they are right or not!

CASE # 15

A couple of years ago, a teen-age girl disappeared back in Canada. She had been in a public place with a girlfriend, and suddenly she was no longer there; no one had seen her leave. She left her coat behind, even though it was a cold evening. A personal object was found a few feet from the building, along with a spot of blood, which the newspapers said was her blood type.

In the third week of November, while working in my kitchen at home, I suddenly felt a spirit come in! I knew it was a young girl, and she was in a total state of confusion and had not gone to the Light. I tried to talk to her telepathically, to help put her over, but she was adamant that she was not going anywhere until she had expressed herself! She was so insistent, that my whole body was vibrating from the confusion, so I turned and walked upstairs to my bedroom where I meditate, and sat down to channel her through.

Before I even sat down, I knew who she was; so I put the tape recorder on, and went into a trance state. It was what we call a medium state of trance; therefore I was conscious of what was transpiring and being said. She was very emotional, and often talked through her sobs. Even though she was confused because of the trauma through which she had been, she gave several details of the things that had happened to her. She was well aware that she had passed, and felt great sadness about leaving her parents whom she loved. I think this was the first time my voice had changed so much during channeling, and it was definitely the voice of a young girl. She left a loving message for her father and mother at the end, and then left my body. I still sensed her around me and I talked to her lovingly, telling her she should go to the Light. But I felt that she planned to stay around to help her parents, and to see that justice was done!

They had found her body in the river a few days earlier, but the autopsy report had not yet come out. I did not mention the tape, or let anyone listen to it, as there were two details she gave which I wanted to compare for my own satisfaction.

Both facts were confirmed through newspaper reports, although the police later said that, because of the body having been in the water for such a long period, it was difficult to really know the cause of death.

Procrastinating because of my own fears, as I usually do in these cases, I really didn't want to do much about it. But she was not to be put off. She kept coming close to me, influencing me to go to the police. Finally I called a friend whose brother is an officer with the Provincial Police, although he works with the drug squad. I have known him for about twenty-five years. He is a special soul, and understands the metaphysical field. One of his closest friends was a well-known American medium, and they always got together when he came to work in Canada. He even took some of his courses at some point. My friend told me that he was in another part of the Province, working on a very large drug case, and only came home on week-ends. I called him at home, and he said it would be better to give the information directly to the homicide squad working on the case.

Preferring to work with someone local, I called the nearest Provincial police. The receptionist put me through to a detective, and the minute he said hello I knew that this was not going to work. I felt a very negative vibration. I took a chance and tried to explain a little; but the moment I mentioned the word "medium", I felt a door closing and his energy shutting down. I asked him for the phone number of the homicide squad in Montreal which was in charge of the case, and he gave it to me. So that was my next step, in spite of my trepidation, because I had made a promise to her.

When I called the city where the crime had been committed, they put me through to one of the detectives working on the case. I liked his vibration, and knew that this was someone who was very humane. I introduced myself, and said that I would be going to the city in a few days; could I meet with him? I explained my background, and he said he didn't know much about these things, but was open to anything. So we made an appointment to meet at his office.

I made a list of some principal facts the spirit had given me, and some details on the murderer, and planned to give these to him. I would let him have more after he checked these out, and I had my proof if I was right or wrong. I had no intention of giving him a copy of the tape until I had my own proof! But at the last minute I was influenced to take the tape with me. I felt her very close, and happy that I was finally moving on this.

I took some information on my work over the years to give to him as credentials. He was quite open, and as nice as he had sounded on the phone. They had received hundreds of tips, many of them from mediums and psychics, but none of them had been right. Many of them supposedly saw her as still being in the physical several days after the abduction, so I guess it was normal for anyone to be a little skeptical about us!

I gave him the list and he looked a little shocked. He said: "If I find **three** of these right, then I'll be a believer!" We chatted for a few minutes. He said that although he had never done it before, he would trust me and let me try to do psychometry on something that had belonged to her. As he left the room to get it, I suddenly felt her presence very strongly; I knew that she had projected herself into the room. She came very close, impressing me with the fact that she wanted to channel through me, and started to take me into a trance state. I knew that there was no way that I would channel her in that office, especially with about twenty detectives sitting at their desks in the big room just outside the door. He walked back in and handed me an object. I was still mentally arguing with her, asking her to move away from me!

The energy used for trance and psychometry, are two completely different types of energy. In the first instance, our consciousness is completely pushed aside and the physical body is taken over by the entity channeling. When this happens, we cannot do other things without creating confusion in our bodies (mental, physical and emotional), which may cause some temporary damage! With psychometry, we center ourselves and go into an altered state. We tune into the energy of the object to pick up what we can from the vibrations. If it is something a person has worn or touched, we can sometimes get their life story.

I held the object and could feel the energy, but I was completely blocked and could not pick up information from it. I stayed very calm, and tried not to feel angry that I had gotten myself into the kind of situation from which I had run away for so long! I tried to explain what was happening in a few words, knowing that he wouldn't be able to understand anyway, and I mentioned that I had the tape. I told the officer that, if he had a tape recorder, I would let him listen to a small part of it. After listening for a few minutes, he asked if I would let him make a copy of it? Once again my fears of being wrong came in; but she was still in the room, and I felt a great sense of inner peace as I agreed to let him keep it. He walked me to the door and gave me his card, telling me to get in touch if I had any more information. The next night, I put him in my meditation. Immediately a scenario came in which I described to him in a letter that I sent a few days before leaving for Florida. He mentioned that sometimes, even though they had all kinds of evidence, proving a case was another story!

When we channel, the information being given is sifted through our subconscious minds. I know I always try to put myself completely aside when I channel, so that what is transpiring will be as pure as possible. I already knew a couple of the details from the newspaper; and when I heard them in my trance state, I thought: "What if they're coming from my subconscious mind?" Once again my great need for perfect truth came back to haunt me! There is only one way to be certain it is the person we think it is, and it is through the intonation of the voice. Even though they are using a voice box which is completely alien to them, they cannot disguise the way a spirit spoke when in the body, unless they wish to do so for a reason. The best way to prove that it is really them, is to let a friend or two listen to a few phrases of the tape, to see if they recognize them through the intonation of the voice.

She came in a couple of times before I left for Florida, and seemed a little depressed. She was often visiting her father and mother, and was sad that in their sorrow they couldn't sense her presence more strongly so that she could console them. No matter how it turns out, I know it was she who channeled through me that day. The fact that I kept my promise to her is the most important part!

Chapter Fourteen

THE SPIRITUAL PATHWAY TODAY

Sometimes someone will ask how I know that life continues after the so called "state of death"; everyone dies, but no one has ever come back to prove it! But I, and millions of people like me who have had a Spiritual awakening, *Know* that we continue living in another dimension. Call it Heaven, the Spirit World, the other side; call it whatever you wish, but it is real!

One of the most concrete examples I can give is one of the experiences Dr. Elizabeth Kubler-Ross, a Swiss born psychiatrist now living in the United States, had a few years ago, and which she shares with her audience when lecturing to Spiritual groups. She has written ten books on her experiences in the field, the first one called "On Death and Dying" which was a best seller. Her wonderful work has helped to dispel the fear of dying for millions of people.

Dr. Kubler-Ross did a great deal of research with patients who were dying or had near death experiences. At one of the lowest points in her life, when she was going through traumatic experiences of her own and was on the verge of giving up her work, one of her patients came to visit. Although she had died six months before, she appeared to the doctor in the flesh. She told Dr. Kubler-Ross that she came back from the Spirit World to tell her that she must not stop her work, that it was imperative that she continue! Dr. Kubler-Ross took her into her office, and they sat down to talk. Being scientifically minded, she asked the Spirit to write a note to another partner in the research, whom this patient had known. What she really wanted was a specimen of her handwriting to compare with her file. This she did, and it was identical to her patient's preceding her death six months before. This shows to what extent the World of Spirit will go to get a message through to someone who is doing some very important work for them on the earth plane. By sending a messenger who materialized in the physical body she wore for so many years, the doctor would *know* that her work on life after death was indeed correct, and that the soul survives after death!

Scientists are beginning to realize more and more that because some things cannot be seen with the physical eyes, or measured, does not mean they don't exist. Humanity has become so "grounded", having lost touch with the Divine side of our being, that we perceive and understand only through the physical senses. Since we descended into matter eons ago, we have long since forgotten our original heritage; that our real home is in the Spirit World. In the beginning of planet earth, we came in our spirit bodies and moved back and forth at will. But as we came to enjoy the pleasures of this planet, we developed a denser body, which matched our new way of thinking. There came a time when we began to forget our real home; and now many of us only go back during the sleep state, when our physical body is at rest, and our astral body can travel "home" for a little visit.

What we don't understand, is that to be able to perceive or sense the Spirit World, we have to be in a completely different state of consciousness. And by refusing to believe, or even consider the possibility of it existing, we eliminate our chances of ever having our proof! By staying open, which does not mean being gullible, we "shift gears" in our consciousness; and we raise our vibrations to where things can start to happen.

We didn't all come in this incarnation to be great mediums. This is not the destiny path for all the souls, for each has his or her own lesson they chose to work on in this lifetime. But even if we only learn to meditate and connect with our higher selves, we can receive our own answers to all life's problems. We make our mistakes when we listen to our lower selves, rather than our "intuition", which is really our higher selves trying to give us the right answers.

Each of us who has had a Spiritual awakening must make the effort to move forward on our pathway quickly, because we will all be called upon to be the "Light bearers" in this wonderful new age of Enlightenment! We are the ones who must put our lower selves aside, and learn to live every moment as our higher, or Spiritual self.

Channeling is the means by which the information from the Spirit World comes to us. Many people are natural channels because of their past life experiences, but for most of us it has to be developed. This can take a short or long period of time, depending on the effort we are ready to make. We need dedication and discipline in our personal lives to take the time necessary each day to meditate, go within, and begin to listen, really listen to the inner silence. This is where it all starts to happen.

If you decide that you really want to serve God in one capacity or another, your beloved Guides in the World of Spirit are waiting patiently to help you develop the Spiritual gifts with which you have been blessed. God gave us free will, so they can only wait for us to open the door. But when we do, we receive much more than we give; and life is never the same again! One of the most important things to remember is to always keep balance in our lives. As Jesus said, "Be *on* the earth, but not *of* the earth". If we are not "grounded", we cannot be a good channel for the Spirit World.

The planet is governed by Universal Law, the most important one being cause and effect. "Whatsoever Ye Sow, So Shall Ye Reap!" Everything in the universe, including mankind, is subject to this Natural Law. All of us are responsible for our own happiness or unhappiness, depending on our attitudes and actions every moment of our lives. If we continually keep a positive attitude, and always expect the best, we automatically attract to us from the Universe all the wonderful things we deserve. We create our own reality! In the past, this creation occurred in our subconscious minds; but in this new age of metaphysics and Spirituality, because of the speeding up of the vibrations on the planet, we create with our conscious minds. We create it by causing it, or allowing it to happen! You enter your personal New Age when you are *ready* to know that you not only create your own reality, but that you do it consciously. No matter what happens in your life, always remember that there is Divine Order in the Universe, and the law is perfect in its operation.

Two of the most important Spiritual Laws are "To Love The God Of Our Own Understanding" and "To Love Our Neighbors As Ourselves". By attaining a high level of Spirituality, and putting it to use in our everyday lives, we recognize that we are one; and everyone and everything in the Universe is connected. If we really understand this, we can never hurt another living thing in any way!

To love others we must first learn to love ourselves! Jesus told us two thousand years ago *To Love Our Neighbor As Ourself*. I believe he meant that unless we love *Ourselves,* we really cannot love anyone else in the right way. But we never understood this message! No one ever taught us that we were supposed to love ourselves. On the contrary, we were brought up to believe that we had to please everyone else, because pleasing ourselves was being selfish. When we learn to really love ourselves from the inside out, and accept ourselves for the unique beings we are, we will begin to understand the meaning of Spirituality, and develop a new relationship with God.

The way to develop this relationship is to meditate and go within. Through meditation, we are able to enter the silence of our being, possibly for the first time in our existence. This means going into our inner world, to the very center of our heart and soul, to find out who we really are. Prayer is talking to God; meditation is letting God talk to us! Not only are we able to reach the source, but it is a state of being in which our family and friends who have gone home to the World of Spirit can reach us with messages of love and encouragement, sustaining us through traumatic periods in our lives. It is also in this space that our beloved Spiritual guides and helpers can contact us to make their presence known.

By going inside ourselves, we are opening that inner door and getting in touch with our souls. This triggers the remembrance of who we really are; the soul with a physical body, its vehicle for this incarnation. The pineal gland, situated at the base of the brain, is our "antenna" to reach the Spirit World, our real home. It takes over in the physical body and starts the flow of energy between the two worlds, so we can receive information from what we always knew as the "unknown world". But it was only unknown to those of us who lived in ignorance, not wishing to understand, because we were too involved in the physical and material world.

My friends, I wish I could tell you that the dark side of life does not exist, and that there is only Light; but it does, and this must be so! Everything that exists in the universe has a polarity. If God exists as a positive energy, as I believe He does, there must be a negative energy almost as strong!

As we move closer to our new Spiritual age, which will herald in one thousand years of peace and harmony on our beloved Mother Earth, there is a great battle being waged with the forces of darkness for the control of the planet. Their greatest weapon is drugs, which are destroying the minds and bodies of our precious children! Some people say that they are winning the battle; but God will never allow this to happen, even though the situation looks very dark at the moment, in many countries. Dr. Kubler-Ross said we were losing a whole generation of young people to this plague, and I wonder if she is not right. Abuse of drugs and alcohol causes a crack in the aura, and this permits negative entities to obsess or possess a person. Because their faculties are being impaired, they, therefore, have no way of protecting themselves from these attacks.

Because of increasing drug and alcohol abuse, we are also seeing more and more of our youngsters becoming involved in satanic rituals and devil worship! While in Florida last winter, I was surprised to learn on the news that many U.S. Police forces have a special department, with officers specially trained to investigate and deal with this problem; and they said it was getting worse! The families of teenagers all over the country are finding evidence that their children are involved in these things, and are turning to the police for help, for they have no where else to go.

I often tell people that **"there is no drug on earth that can give you the "*High*" that Spirituality can!"** By keeping our thoughts loving and balanced, we continually keep everything in perspective and can handle anything life gives us. Turning to drugs can destroy the mind and our whole existence; and we often end up losing everything!

To those of you who have been touched by the experiences in this book, I want to say: "Do not fear the future!" As the soul, you have *CHOSEN* to be here at this most crucial time in the history of humanity. We are on the brink, standing on the threshold of a whole new world! You wanted to share in the excitement and joy of the Dawning Of The New Age Of Aquarius, bringing with it a new Spirituality. It is closing the door to the old, and really awakening to a new world, when every race and creed shall walk hand in hand on the pathway of self-realization. *A time when the lion shall lay down with the lamb, which will herald in one thousand years of peace and harmony. A time when we shall know the true meaning of unconditional love, and our connection to every living thing in the Universe. A time when we shall turn back to care for our beloved Mother Earth and appreciate her as the Living Being from which all sustenance comes, and without whom mankind cannot survive.*

Jesus said, "Not even a little bird shall fall unless my Father knows about it", and "Every hair on your head is counted". This should tell us that there is a Divine Power in control of the planet; and each of us has a very special place in the tapestry of the cosmic plan, which is *"To Restore Heaven On Earth, As it Was Originally Meant To Be"*.

The Golden Ray of Christ Consciousness energy of unconditional love has been anchored very strongly into the planet; and the message that Christ came to Earth to bring two thousand years ago, and was not understood, is coming around again. He stands at the door of our hearts and knocks. We only have to open the door to receive. The message that he came to bring was "To Love God As Our Spiritual Father; To Love Our Neighbor As Ourself; And To Tell Us That *All The Things He Did Two Thousand Years Ago, Which Were Considered "Miracles", We Could Do; And Even Greater Things Shall We Do!"*

To all of you who have had an awakening of the soul through the reading of this book, I say to you: "Go! Take your rightful place in the Universe as the Divine Being that you are! Walk the pathway with love in your hearts, and spread the Light to all your brothers and sisters on the planet who are thirsting for knowledge and understanding. Know that we are all one, no matter the race, color or creed; we are all God's beloved children, many of whom have temporarily lost their way but will soon be turning back to be embraced by our Creator once again. And don't forget the love for the animal kingdom; because everything that exists in the Universe, from the smallest bug crawling on the ground or flying in the air, to the beautiful galaxy of stars we admire above us on a clear summer night, is connected through Divine energy. May you walk your pathway with joy in your hearts, and I leave each of you with **"Love, Light, Peace And Joy"**, **and a Special Blessing From The Father/Mother God.** I also leave you with a poem that the Spirit World inspired me to write three years ago.

––––––––––

CARRY THE TORCH HIGH

Every day that I live, challenges are placed before me; big ones and small ones, depending on the soul growth needed that day. Each new day is like picking up the Olympic Flame for a new run that will last all eternity.

I can carry it high with joy in my heart, knowing my strength will grow with each victory won; or I can lay it down and refuse to go forward, accepting the deceptions that life gives me with a heavy heart, not realizing that I created these obstacles because I **needed** them to advance on my soul path with greater strength and clarity.

I am the only one responsible for my life! Whether I am happy or unhappy depends on my philosophy of life. **What I sow, I must reap; that is God's Great Law of Cause and Effect!**

I pray each day that God will give me the strength to continue, so that I may learn perfect faith.

ORDER FORM

That's The Spirit Publishing Company

In the United States:

> P.O. Box 2503
> Ft Lauderdale, Fl 33303-2503
> Tel: (305) 522-8317

In Canada:

> Suite 226
> 1568 Merivale Road
> Nepean, Ontario K2G 5Y7
> Tel: (613) 825-0259

— —

Please send me ___ copies of *SOUL RESCUE*
Help on the Way Home to Spirit.

In U.S.:   I have enclosed $12.95 for each book,
plus $3.50 P&H for the first book,
and $1.00 for each additionnal copy.

In Canada: $15.95 plus $4.00 P&H for first book
and $1.50 for each additional copy.

Name: _____

Address: _____

City: _____ State/Prov._____ Zip/Code_____

Phone: (___) _____-_____

Please send me ___copies of *SOUL RESCUE*
                                    Help on the Way Home to Spirit.

In U.S.:   I have enclosed $12.95 for each book,
              plus $3.50 P&H for the first book,
              and $1.00 for each additionnal copy.

In Canada: $15.95 plus $4.00 P&H for first book
              and $1.50 for each additional copy.

Name: _____

Address: _____

City: _____ State/Prov._____Zip/Code_____

Phone: (___) _____-_____

- -

ORDER FORM

That's The Spirit Publishing Company

In the United States:

> P.O. Box 2503
> Ft Lauderdale, Fl 33303-2503
> Tel: (305) 522-8317

In Canada:

> Suite 226
> 1568 Merivale Road
> Nepean, Ontario K2G 5Y7
> Tel: (613) 825-0259